13 Steps To Evil
Superbad

By Sacha Black

Copyright

13 Steps To Evil – How To Craft Superbad Villains

Copyright © 2017 Sacha Black

First Published May 2017, by Atlas Black Publishing

Edited by: Esther Newton, Editing and Advice Service
Cover design: Andrew Brown, Design for Writers

www.sachablack.co.uk

Contents Page

For all the writers with a glint in their eye.

Read Me First

Heroes are interesting. But mostly they're predictable. They save the world and win. Again, and again, and again. If the constant monotony of halo-polishing heroism has worn you as thin as it has me, then you're in the right place. I am tired of stifling yawns and waking up in my book's spine because nothing chuffing happened in the story. Where's the tension, people? Where's the grit, the emotion, and the conflict?

It's *'nice'* to write a chivalrous, charming, debonair or dashingly handsome hero who never fails. I mean, who doesn't want to be swept off their feet? But let's be honest. Heroes aren't the fun ones to write. It's much more satisfying to craft a character with an evil glint in their eye. Someone who's so unpredictable even you don't know what they'll do next. That's why a villain will always be the most delicious character to write.

Do you want a story that grips your readers? A story with depth and the juiciest, most bad ass villain in town to give your stories that extra edge? Then I can help.

As writers, you're expected to create complex and unique characters while remaining true to the tropes of your genre. But that's getting harder, and readers, the bastards, aren't making it easier for us. They're more intelligent. They've read more books in your genre than you could if you didn't do anything else between now and the day you died. Worse, they're quicker to figure out your sinister twists, because they've seen it, read it and heard it all before.

If you're reading this, my guess is you fit into one of the following categories:

- Your villain isn't cutting the evil mustard.
- You're a halo-wearing angel at heart and couldn't possibly write a dark and twisted villain.
- You already wrote a villain, but they were clichéd, sporting a moustache and using a 'muhaha' retro styled laugh.
- You just want to write better characters.
- You're a villain virgin and would rather like to pop your evil cherry.
- You know me personally and wondered what the fudge I've been doing for the last two years squirreled away all antisocial with a laptop for a BFF.

If you fit into any of those categories, this book will help. It will teach you to craft villains so brilliantly twisted they'll make your readers throw themselves like sacrificial lambs between the pages of your book.

Readers love to hate villains. They're word-fish swimming suicidally towards your story hook and all so they can be dragged to the verge of sympathizing with your villain only to be horrified when they realize he's so cruel and nefarious they couldn't possibly have sympathized with him. Only we know they did because we designed our villain that way.

During explanations in this book, I predominantly use the term villain. Villains and antagonists *are* different, and I do explain why, shortly. But, for the sake of simplicity, I'll stick to villain. Just apply whichever term is most relevant to your story.

If you've come to this book hoping for a list of villains to suit every type of story, you'll be disappointed. The point of the next forty thousand words is to give you the tools you need to craft the right villain for the right plot. But I will use a range of top notch villains from a variety of examples to show you how you can.

The first part of this book is focused solely on developing the best villain possible. You'll learn about traits, motives, goals, how to create a credible and authentic villain, as well as how to curate a backstory that will leave your readers desperate for more. We'll also dissect anti-heroes and spend some time learning how to spot, as well as avoid, villainous clichés.

The last part of the book focuses on the more complex aspects of villains touching upon mental health and commonly portrayed disorders that villains often have as well as examining how to create conflict, set up your climax and showdown as well as touching on fear and phobias.

If you read 13 Steps To Evil cover to cover, you'll learn everything you need to create your perfect villain from the ground up. But I've tried to add enough detail to each step that should you want to skip parts and use it like a reference book, you can. But don't, cause it'll make me sad, and I hate being sad.

Think of this book as Yoda; it will give you tools, questions and prompts to help you think about and develop the best villain for your genre and your story. But like Obi-Wan, you'll need to go practice with the 'evil'-force if you want to master your villains.

If you want to sell the books you bleed, then you'll also need to know your market and that, young pad wan, you'll have to research alone. You need to be at one with your genre; merge with it like a big white fluffy polar bear camouflaged in the Arctic. Readers read genres for a reason; it's like going home for them. They know what's behind the first-page-front-door and there are certain things villains from their hometown will, and won't do. You need to know these things because there's a cocktail of nuances and tropes in each genre. Some you can bat away like dead flies; others your readers will expect you to adhere to and if you don't, the villain police will come and arrest you, you traitorous heathen, you. Okay, that's a lie. There are no villain police, but the readers will expect you to adhere to some tropes.

If that sounds terrifying, then fear not, I've stolen E.T's big fat phosphorescent finger and used it to point you in the right direction - the summaries will help, and the important stuff's summarized in there.

Before we start, let's make sure you're going to get what you need. **There are four reasons you should stop reading now:**

One: If you're here to learn about writing horror, then stop now; thank you for picking this book up, but it's not for you. I am not a horror writer, and although many aspects of villainy are translatable to horror, this book is devoted to villains more broadly. It's been constructed purposely using well-known examples from a range of genres, films, books and TV so that it's suitable for writers of any genre.

Two: You write literary fiction or fiction that doesn't easily sit in a genre. Most of the examples in this book come from genre fiction. While you may be able to take elements of the lessons from this book into general fiction, I don't cover it specifically.

Three: If you're sensitive in any way, don't like bad words, odd explanations, or dodgy humor, you might wanna leave before things get ugly.

Four: In order to give high quality examples to illustrate how to create superbad villains, there are story plots and therefore spoilers littered throughout the book. I've tried to keep to very well-known books and films, to lower the risk of spoilers, but you never know so it's only fair I tell you now.

Still with me? Then welcome on board.

Let's get our villain on.

STEP 1 –Villainy 101

Screw Superman, Your Novel Needs A Lex Luthor Love-in

Every writer, at some point in their book writing career, has a secret love affair with their hero or protagonist, and if it's not the dashing protagonist we writers swoon over, then it's his or her love interest. As soon as we ink those first words on the page, a festival of love-ins and hero worship begins.

Tut, tut. We writers have been foolish. Why didn't our word-mothers ever teach us the hero doesn't matter? Maybe it will come as a surprise to you, but for the sake of your novel, you ought to know…

Your hero is *not* the most important character in your novel.

Your villain is.

I know. Don't freak out; it's a truth I found hard to accept too. But believe me, *it is true.* Think about it:

Would Metropolis have needed Superman in all his glorious Lycra-wearing amazingness if it weren't for Lex Luthor and his plans for world domination? Probably not. Old Clark K would have knocked up Lois Lane quick-time as they created their version of unfairly attractive mini-mes in a suburban nightmare.

There's a meme on the internet that says behind every successful man, is a woman. Let's flip that on its head.

Behind every successful hero, is a villain.

Let me ask you a question: *What is the most important aspect when constructing a novel?*

Some writers are long-term supporters of the plot camp, others the character camp. Both are important, but I'd argue for something more fundamental than either plot or characters. To me, the most important aspect of a novel is:

Conflict

Without conflict, you have nothing. Your plot and characters flat line beyond the help of any crash cart. **The plot is based on conflict. No conflict, no plot.** If there's no conflict, there's nothing to make your characters change or grow through their character arc, which means there are no characters either.

Let's look at a couple of examples.

Example: Harry Potter and the Philosopher's Stone by J.K. Rowling - The main conflict comes from a prophecy made by Professor Trelawney: a boy born at the end of July will defeat the Dark Lord Voldemort. There's your conflict: a prophecy of defeat.
This creates the need for a boy character, (born at the appropriate time, Harry), for the evil wizard Voldemort to hunt and kill so he can prevent the prophecy occurring. But, oh, the irony. Voldemort is a self-fulfilling prophecy, because going after Harry is what puts him in a six-foot hole before the first novel starts, and so the world of Harry Potter begins.

*Example: **Romeo and Juliet** by **William Shakespeare*** - Two families are at war. Therefore, love and relationships between the families are forbidden.

This creates the characters (Romeo from one family and Juliet from the other) and the plot: Romeo and Juliet falling in love with each other without knowing who the other is.

From conflict, derives your plot and all your characters.

Heroism doesn't come cheap; heroes have to work for their book pages. And that's where your villain comes in. To have a hero, you need some tentacle-faced super villain to stand in their way (even if the villain's an intangible hatred between Romeo and Juliet's families).

Your villain's wants and needs create conflict for your hero and your story is the tale of who wins: hero or tentacle face? Because their goals conflict, the tale will result in repeated twisty-turny, head bashing, blood spilling conflict. That is action, and it drives the plot forward keeping the reader gripped to the page.

Without someone opposing your hero and creating conflict, there isn't a need for the hero, which means there isn't a story either.

Villain Engineering - The Plot Device

In technical terms, villains are little literary troublemakers also known as a 'plot device.'

And a plot device is any mechanism within a book that moves the plot forward.

Your villain needs to be a plot-thorn in your hero's ass. His goals should oppose or threaten your hero's because it creates conflict and everybody loves a scandal. He also needs to pursue his goal, with as much forehead creasing determination as your hero does.

Add A Sprinkle of Villains And A Dash Of Antagonists

The words villain and antagonist get thrown around interchangeably like stolen booze in a teenage nightclub. But villains are not the same as antagonists. They are not mutually exclusive.

An antagonist is a character or thing that opposes the protagonist (or hero). A villain *is* an antagonist because they oppose the hero. But *an antagonist does not have to be a villain.*

A villain indicates some level of evil while an antagonist does not.

For example, if you write non-fiction memoirs you're more likely to find a real-life **antagonist** because the stories are personal. But in a fiction book about gangsters, you're liable to find **villains** because they commit crimes and hurt people.

This is one of those writer things that can create blurred edges and a lot of word-fog, so let's continue using Harry Potter as an example because it has both villains and antagonists:

Lord Voldemort is, without a doubt, a villain; he is one evil momma-Potter killer who regularly commits unspeakable acts of evil.

Draco Malfoy, however, while teetering on the edge of evil, never quite makes it. He's more of a nuisance to Harry, like when you're making fajitas and rub chili in your eye. It's bloody annoying and stings like a bitch, but it won't kill you. Draco Malfoy is an antagonist.

One Part Hero To Two Parts Protagonist

Let's give ourselves déjà vu: like villains and antagonists, heroes and protagonists are not the same either. While the majority of novels use the same character for the protagonist as the hero, not all do.

Protagonists are the subject of the story – it's who the book is about. But the hero is someone of extraordinary ability (albeit not necessarily magic powers) who does good things.

Batman is a non-magical classic hero. He's a normal guy who happens to be kick ass because he saves a bunch of people's lives by beating the crappits out of the bad ones.

But your hero doesn't have to be a kid's cartoon cut out superhero. He could just as easily be the neighbor who runs into the road in front of a car to save your protagonist's suicidal dog. Or the money mogul who sees the light and decides she can't be fulfilled unless she gives away her fortune.

It's becoming more popular for novels to have an anti-hero for a protagonist, but more on anti-heroes in STEP 7.

In *The Silence of the Lambs*, Hannibal Lecter is a villain, but he is also the protagonist. The story is about him, and what he did, but the hero of the story is Clarice Starling, an FBI agent trying to solve the crimes of another serial killer.

Gone Girl has two protagonists: a couple, one of whom turns out to be the villain.

Why Writers Fudge Up Their Villains

Villains are like newborn infants. So much glorious potential. Until we writers get our grubby mitts on them and balls it up. With the careless flick of a pen, we can turn a finely sculpted baby villain into a cringe-worthy cliché because we didn't make him bad enough, or we create something so heinously evil it's unrealistic.

A villain might be a plot device, but he still needs a purpose and a goal, or he's unworthy as an opponent for your hero (See STEP 3 for motives and goals).

While researching this book, writers told me all kinds of problems they encountered while creating their villains. From getting the dialogue right and avoiding clichés, to knowing how evil to make a villain, to how to reveal her motives without using blatant exposition.

Behind all these issues lie two basic barriers that are the Achilles in every writer's villainous heel:

1. **Depending on the point of view (POV) the book's written in, the villain is *usually* seen through the eyes of your hero.**

A solitary POV gives you a page-limited amount of time to show your villain's best, most authentic and devilishly evil side. Page-limited to the point it makes it eye-wateringly difficult to convey her backstory effectively without information dumping. You have to be better, clearer, more tactical and more concise with your words to create superbad villains.

2.   **Writers are hero worshippers**.

We love our heroes and protagonists more than our spouses. And as a result, we spend shameful amounts of time honing our protagonist's muscular heroics into shape. But that relegates our villain (the plot-driving conflict-creator) to the corner of our book, complete with a nobody-loves-you-anyway hat. In other words, writers don't pay enough attention to their villain.

And Now For Something A Little Philosophical

Let me prod your morally inclined cells with a few questions. When you take that first life-giving sip of coffee in the morning sat in front of the news, and you see the same depression-inducing stories you've heard over and over again, have you ever asked yourself when you became numb?

We watch the news like it's a re-run of a classic *Friends* episode. With barely a passing interest and only the occasional flicker of an eyebrow when something mildly controversial is covered. But the news is full of more dark nastiness than one of my son's soiled nappies.

We are saturated with bad news. It's thrown at us multiple times a day whether it's the news, through advertising or the photoshopped bodies in magazines, and because of it, what we used to think of as wrong: children before marriage or wrists and ankles on show, is now laughable. Our definition of 'bad' has changed immeasurably.

To write a good villain, (and by good, I mean superbad) dictionary definitions and your trusty pocket guide to psychopaths aren't good enough anymore.

You need to decide what 'wrong' and 'evil' mean to you because society is going to keep changing its mind.

If a mother steals a loaf of bread for her starving child is that wrong or evil? Most would say no. But what if she took it from a struggling shopkeeper? What if that theft made his business go into liquidation and his wife left him then he committed suicide? Does that make what she did wrong or evil?

The answer doesn't matter. One character's immoral actions could be another's survival. What's important is drawing out some semblance of a personal philosophy. Would you have stolen the bread?

What if you don't know how much evil is too evil? Or are you worried your villain only hits the pint-sized mark on the evil measuring stick of doom?

Then find your morally inclined line and figure out if you're chucking your villain over it or not.

Unless you're a bona fide sociopath, the likelihood is your moral balance beam isn't that different to the rest of us. Use your morals as a villain-compass, point north for bread thieving mommas and south for frothy demons guarding the gates of hell.

STEP 1 – Villain 101 Summary

Remember, screw Superman, it's all about Lex Luthor. The most important part of your novel is the conflict. And conflict is derived from your villain. So, give your villain the appropriate care and attention he needs.

- Without conflict, your book, plot and characters will flat line. Your book needs it like you need oxygen.

- The difference between a villain and an antagonist is that a villain is evil, an antagonist isn't, but they both oppose the hero.

- The difference between a hero and a protagonist is that a hero has a superhuman ability for good, whereas the protagonist is who the story is about.

- Your hero doesn't have to be your protagonist, and your villain doesn't have to be your antagonist.

- The cause of most villain weaknesses can be traced back to two mistakes:

1. The lack of page time a villain gets because most books are written from the perspective of a hero.

2. Underdeveloped villains and the lack of attention a writer has given them while developing their novel.

- Use your personal philosophy and morals as a beacon, a guiding light you can utilize to define how evil your villain is.

Questions To Think About

Think of the villain in your genre. Can you identify the examples where the villain is the protagonist, or perhaps an antagonist rather than a villain?

I mentioned *Gone Girl* and *The Silence of the Lambs* as two examples where the protagonist was not the hero. Can you think of any more examples from any genre and what about the genre you write in?

STEP 2 - The Perfect Traits for the Perfect Villain

People, generally speaking, are the culmination of mess, confusion and chaos. Even stood in front of someone staring all squinty eyed in concentration, it can still be hard to figure out who they are and what's at their core.

That's because humans are a cauldron of emotions and behaviors. But as confusing as we are, more often than not, we react in extremely predictable ways to things.

That behavioral consistency is what allows us to get to know one another and build relationships.

Did you have a friend at college or school who always sat at the front of a class? The one who had to answer every question? Maybe you know someone who picks their nose while driving precariously fast down country roads. Or maybe you know that guy who can't help but be a knight in shining armor to every woman with legs and functioning lungs.

Humans are creatures of habit, especially when it comes to our personalities. We're consistent until suddenly, we're not. But that's what makes us special, we change our minds and are spontaneous, when others least expect it.

Behaving out of character is 'out of character' for a reason. It's an extreme reaction to something out of the blue. Like when the little 104lb mother rips a twisted, burning car door off its hinges to save her baby.

Example: The Red Queen by Victoria Aveyard - The Red Queen is set in a world with magical royals and a slave population without powers. There are two prince half-brothers, Cal and his half-brother Maven. Maven's always lived in Cal's shadow, and he always appeared to be fine with that, until the day the crown is handed to Cal and then Maven snaps and so becomes the villain.

Your plot should push a character to behave out of the norm; it's part of a character's arc. In the first half of a story, characters (especially the hero and the villain) are consistent: they behave as you created them and do as they're told because the plot does stuff *to* them, almost like they are victims of your plot. In the first half, your characters are simply puppets in your masterfully woven stories.

But something in your book, usually around the middle, should change your characters. Something forces your hero to stop being a victim of the plot, and to be proactive. This is what leads to your character changing and pushes your story to its climax.

Characters need consistent behaviors because it makes their spontaneous reactions even more surprising to both the other characters and the reader. These spontaneous reactions, and changes in personality, help you develop depth as well as conflict.

But for your character to have an abnormal reaction to something, you first have to establish what his 'normal' behaviors are. That's where traits come in.

Traits are the parts of personality that produce consistent behavior.

Dictionary.com defines a trait as:

A distinguishing feature belonging to a person.

Traits are both the stuff you flaunt: like momma being proud of you for winning the sports trophy at school, as well as the secret flaws you'd rather bury. Like the real reason you won the trophy is because you're dating your sports teacher.

These behaviors are caused by the traits that sit at the core of you and your characters. They are the seeds in your personality apples. Likewise, they're the aspects of your character's personality that give him a unique flair making him rise as a hero or fall into the pit of villainy.

Writers pour energy into thinking about what traits their heroes have but then ignore their villains. Is it any wonder they get pissy and choke out a clichéd laugh for you?

Avoiding your villain's personality is wrong. Super freaking wrong. Having one-dimensional villains with one 'angry, world ending' trait is going to leave your novel as flat as a squashed pancake, your villain unbelievable and your hero weak.

Traits can be positive or negative. I've included three lists in the appendix: Positive Traits, Negative Traits and Neutral Traits. But, for a full guide on positive and negative traits that goes into the nitty gritty detail of how to write them correctly, I recommend **The Positive Trait Thesaurus** and **The Negative Trait Thesaurus** by Angela Ackerman and Becca Puglisi.

Examples of positive traits include: Adaptable, Charming, Decisive, Merciful, Leader, Trusting.

Examples of negative traits include: jealous, reckless, greedy, possessive, addictive, cowardly.

But There Are SO Many Traits

Real people, you know, the squishy, pudgy miserable skin sacks you sit opposite at work, have dozens of traits. People are complicated, but then we have a lifetime to develop and display our traits.

We might display behaviors from a huge range of traits, but each of us has a unique handful we show more regularly than any others; these are our consistent behaviors - the core of our personality. The things that people would say if you asked them to describe you in three words.

You're real. But your characters, while they might pitch a screaming fit in your mind when you don't pay attention, are not.

I hate to break it to you, but those voices...are in your head. And the bodies attached to them live between the knitted words adorning your creamy book paper and cardboard covers. I know, I know. Hearing that pains me too, especially because those characters are my only friends, but come on now. Eventually, we have to accept they aren't real and acknowledge we don't have limitless amounts of time to make our readers believe our characters are as flabby, squishy and skin sacky as you or I.

But that's okay because this is fiction. Not realism. Readers aren't expecting real humans to climb out the pages and act out the story in a display of thespian Shakespearianism. **Readers know books aren't real. They just need enough depth for characters to be a reflection of reality.**

You don't have time to accurately portray your villain as a multifaceted *human* with a plethora of traits. So, don't try. If you do, and you're not writing *War and Peace* Mark

II, you'll end up with a wishy-washy, inconsistent, unbelievable villain who's not much of anything.

Better to have a small handful of traits that pack the power of a literary atom bomb than try to capture the essence (like for like) of humanity's complexity.

Choose a couple of traits for your villain and show them consistently; it gives you the time to create a greater depth of character. It also means that when your villain pushes the right buttons and makes your hero behave out of character it will be much more believable. That's why traits for both your hero and your villain are so important.

Yeah, But What Traits Should A Villain Have?

Choosing what traits a character should have is super fun because you get to play God. It's the best part of being a writer. You're in the big leagues of people creation.

Because villains get so little page time, you have to go big or go home, but going 'big' doesn't necessarily mean shooting straight for the big bad serial killing psychopath traits.

What it means, is that **when you create your villain, whatever traits you do show, need to be in your face**. Like a red-light district's glowing streets only louder and with big red fire truck sirens that blast 'come get me, sugar' in your reader's face.

As soon as your villain enters the story, show the reader who they are, whether that's tactless, stupid, arrogant or the quiet villain who consistently displays sinister traits. **Consistency creates character.**

Your villain doesn't have to be intent on destroying the world; she just has to want to nut your hero in his precious parts. Unless it's unavoidable (or you write crime), don't smash readers over the head with the obvious villain-psychopath-anvil. Go for more subtle and nuanced traits, because that makes for a far more realistic villain.

Answer The Bloody Question - What Traits Should A Villain Have?

You know those really vague rambling paragraphs that instead of telling you the answer like you wanted just ask a lot of questions... yeah, sorry for that. But there aren't any hard and fast rules to picking traits.

I do, however, have three tips to help you choose wisely:

Tip 1: Don't have a villain without at least one negative trait.

Choose a minimum of one but usually a couple of negative traits for your villain. Whether it's arrogance, greed, power hunger, or cowardliness, you need to include one, ideally more.

Tip 2: Include at least one positive trait.

To make a villain realistic, and to get your readers to love to hate them, include at least one positive trait or redeeming quality. It's a weird concept, a villain with redeeming qualities, but it is a necessity. After all, even villains have mommies.

Tip 3: Pick whatever traits you want, but bear trait polarity in mind.

Trait polarity has two sides: a hero and a villain with similar traits, or with opposing traits. Both are beneficial story tactics; you just have to decide what fits your story better.

Opposites Attract For The Right Reasons

Why should your hero have opposing traits to your villain? **Because it drives conflict.**

If your hero is charming and diplomatic and your villain is tactless, he will grate like nails down a chalkboard on your hero. And like magic, you have successfully created conflict.

If your villain has traits that are in direct conflict to your hero's, you create character marmite; they're either going to love or hate each other. At their core, heroes and villains are as different as the flavors of jellybeans. Like conservative vs liberal, republican vs democrat. Opposing traits will provoke ferocious battles that your characters will lay down their lives for.

Opposing core traits between villain and hero mean they will fight not only over the big, world destroying stuff but the simplest of things too.

Example: Mean Girls, The Movie - The protagonist, Cady Heron, is the new weird kid who lived in sub-Saharan Africa for most of her life. She has an open mind and is a kind, non-materialistic person. The antagonist is a superficial, closed-minded bitch of a queen bee called Regina George. Regina's ex-boyfriend falls for the new girl Cady because she's everything Regina isn't. And so, a high school war commences.

Peter Pan and Captain Hook are diametrically opposed. Hook is old; Peter is eternally young. Hook is boring and mature; Peter is full of fun and immature.

As well as opposing the hero and villain's traits, you can do the same to their individual positive and negative traits.

Character Example: Hannibal Lecter from Silence of the Lambs by Thomas Harris- Hannibal is a serial killing psychopath, but he also happens to be a bit of a charming gentleman when it comes to Clarice.

So much so, for the briefest of moments, you wonder what Clarice really thinks and feels about him. At the end of the film, he's still a cannibal, and she's still a cop. Nonetheless, **the conflicting traits create not just action related conflict, but internal conflict for Clarice, both of which drive the plot.**

Heroes and villains with opposing traits make sense. It fills the reader with the soothing comfort of logic. It gives them literary chills, like the time you experimented with ice cream 'just to see.'

Diametrically opposed heroes and villains are awesome, but there's another trick that works just as well:

Making them the same.

Same, Same Only, Well...Different

Wait, what? You can make your hero and villain the same? Yes. Yes, you can.

No really. Your hero and villain don't need to be separated by an ocean of trait-errific differences. Think about it, having different traits isn't what defines a villain or a hero. In fact, traits don't define any of us. **What defines us is our reaction and subsequent choices to different situations**, but I talk more about that in STEP 4.

If you have two characters that are similar and faced with the same choice then all that separates them is their actions and reactions to that situation. We know villains make bad choices, and it's only in these situations when a hero with a similar personality makes an alternative choice that we see the difference.

Example: Thor and Loki from the Marvel Universe - Although not genetic brothers, Thor and Loki were brought up by the same parents, as princes.

The brothers are both obscenely arrogant, have god complexes, and the desire to lead their kingdom. They are, despite physical appearances, remarkably similar. And yet, when faced with the opportunity to have the crown, Thor thrives and pushes his arrogance aside to prove his worth and Loki fails, letting his ego consume him and lead him to make terrible choices that ultimately cost him the one thing he wants: the crown.

When a hero and villain have similar personalities it's the similarity that makes the differences in action so stark.

Everybody Loves To Hate A Villain

The best villains, are those we love to hate. There's nothing better than loving a villain who rips your heart out after doing something awful to the hero's pet hamster, and then finding you kind of still like them anyway. Producing that emotional rollercoaster is a skill, an art form, and it creates reader rocket fuel.

Make the reader feel for your villain, sympathize with their craziness and agree with their insane ideas for just one second and then slap them back to reality with a side salad of villain crazy. **Because making a reader empathize with a villain before doing something awful makes the emotional turmoil much more compelling**. But beware, pull the wool over their eyes, yes, but don't trick them so they're left feeling cheated.

Readers don't like to be cheated. If you set your villain up to make the reader empathize with him early on, be sure to plant a seed of doubt in their mind about his 'goodness.'

I've mentioned earlier that you need to give your villain at least one redeeming or positive quality because a positive trait = realism.

There's nothing worse than a character who's evil for the sake of it. No one is evil for the sake of it. That's an exaggeration you can only get away with in very young children's books, and even in Disney films the villains have a redeeming quality.

Giving your bad guy at least one positive trait creates balance for all their negative ones, and with balance comes realism and believability.

Even one-track mind, world ending villains like Lord Voldemort have positive traits.

Character Example: Lord Voldemort from the Harry Potter series by J.K. Rowling - As Tom Riddle, he is charming (albeit the charm is used to manipulate) and handsome. As Voldemort, he is patient and intelligent.

This, although you never really like him, makes you feel at least a teeny bit sorry for the mess Tom ends up in. It gives depth to his character, a human side to his evil Voldemort persona and that makes him relatable. After all, people aren't all good or all bad and neither should your villains be.

The book's theme is also important; it helps to pull that silk thread through your book connecting the start with the end and everything in between.

Where your readers love the hero because he embodies your book's theme, the villain must represent the anti-theme, or the opposing quality to your book's theme.

Character Example: Katniss in The Hunger Games by Suzanne Collins - Katniss embodies the book's theme: self-sacrifice by taking the place of her sister in the Reaping (an event likely to kill her sister). But President Snow (the villain) is the exact opposite. The only thing he ever sacrifices is other people.

Reasons Are Reality, But Morals Will Do Too

Villain: "I want to destroy the world…"
Hero: "Okay, but why?"
Villain: "Because I do…"
Hero: "Right."

Not only is that terrible dialogue, it sounds pathetic, doesn't it? That's because you need to give your villain **a reason** to want to destroy the world. Not just because 'they do.' No one (unless they're three years old) will accept 'because I said so' as justification for ending the world. It simply isn't valid because it's not how people work. All 'because I do' creates, is a villain that appears clichéd.

Aside from the right reasoning, giving your villain morals not only makes them insane, it makes their thinking appear more justifiable to the reader.

A villain with morals not only thinks what they are doing is right, they think it's justified and for the greater good of everyone else, and that's terrifying.

It also makes it more of an emotional upheaval for your protagonist to kill the villain if he isn't all evil. Maybe your villain's kind to his sidekick, or a pet – Voldemort has a snake (Nagini) that he loves. Loving another thing, whether it be a villain's mom, a creature or a child, creates a redeeming quality, and that produces depth, authenticity, and complexity.

Weepy Little Villain

Traits create personality which produces reactions to events. **Reactions = emotions.**

Whether it's anger, frustration, or hurt, villains should display emotions just like your hero and supporting characters. Your villain doesn't need to be a sniveling bag of wimp that tears up every time Oprah comes on. But he does have to show *a range of* emotion, no matter how small.

If your villain can be hurt, because his one positive trait is caring for his pipsqueak henchman, then it's a conflict enabler and your hero probably ought to know about his weakness.

Emotions drive plot. They are tied to old personal wounds. They create weaknesses which mean blind spots. Blind spots mean a hero can exploit it and use it to kick the villain's booty into prison.

Example: Thor and Loki from the Marvel Universe - In *Thor*, Loki's flaw is that he would do anything to get the Asgard crown because he wants to prove himself a worthy son to his father. See - makes sense, right? His flaws derive from his emotion and his love for his father. His bad decision and descent into villainy occur because his father hurts him, and he's reacting to that hurt.

The hero always has to make a sacrifice to defeat the villain. But it should be no different for the villain. If the Evil Queen wants to defeat Snow White, it can't be easy for her either.

STEP 2 – The Perfect Traits for the Perfect Villain Summary

Humans are messy and confusing, but more often than not, we react predictably to events because we are creatures of habit.

- We're consistent until suddenly, we're not. But that's what makes us unique; we're spontaneous. But, to have a different reaction to something, you first have to establish character and normal behaviors through traits.

- The facets of personality that produce consistent behavior are called traits.

- You write fiction, not realism. Readers aren't expecting real humans to climb out the pages because they know books aren't real. They need just enough depth for characters to be a reflection of reality.

- You don't have time to accurately portray your villain as a multifaceted human. So, don't try.

- A small handful of traits used consistently will pack the power of a literary atom bomb.

- Three tips for picking traits:

  Tip 1: You can't have a villain without at least one negative trait.

  Tip 2: You need to include at least one positive trait.

  Tip 3: Pick whatever traits you want, but

bear trait polarity in mind.

- Opposing core traits between villain and hero is a good tactic, but so is giving them the *same* traits. You can also oppose his or her individual positive and negative traits too.

- Readers don't like to be cheated so if you set your villain up for readers to sympathize with him early on, plant clues to his evil inner core.

- Where your hero encompasses the theme, the villain must represent the anti-theme.

- A villain with morals not only thinks what she's doing is right, she believes it's justified and for the greater good of everyone, and that's scary.

Questions To Think About

Think about some of your favorite villains in your genre. What mix of traits do they have? What's the balance between positive and negative traits?

Who or what does your villain love? What is their redeeming quality? And how can your hero manipulate it to win?

STEP 3 - Motivating Your Goals

Of all the words we learn as children, one tops the 'really bloody annoying' chart.

Why?

When a kid learns the meaning of the word 'why,' it's the equivalent of knifing the parent in the stomach, chucking their twisted innards on the floor and watching them seethe in a mass of parental horror and confusion. At that moment, children learn the art of manipulation.

But why also spawns myriad other headache–inducing problems for parents like independent decision making (the pint-sized heathens) and outright toddler rebellions (the swines). The word why causes the tiny homunculi to realize the world does not revolve around them.

Why causes kids to question everything including you, Gammy, the dog, the postman and anything with a remotely steady heartbeat, including themselves. And that means they decide whether or not they want to do something, like obey the ~~slaves~~ parents.

But what in the name of royal wordery do toddler tantrums have to do with creating superbad villains?

A Sprinkle Of This, A Splash Of That, Bake For 80,000 Words And Hey Presto, Motive Cake

The word why is the source of all personality.

Why sits behind every author's story creation. It's what makes us get up in the morning and what causes us to fall in love.

Why gives us our purpose, our motivations and our goals.

Why is the driver at the core of our soul. Think of it as NASA's home brew for personality rocket fuel. It powers behavior, desires, and ambitions. I'd bet my left nipple you know your hero's motives, as well as you know your own reason for getting up in the morning. But I'd also bet my right one on the fact you haven't given as much time to your villain's motives.

And yet, your slippery villain needs a motive as much as your squeaky-clean hero does. If anything, you need to spend a little more time developing your villain's motives than your hero's.

I've no doubt you could multitask like a pro, take a leak, eat a full roast dinner and catch Pokémon Go while deciding your hero's motives. Save the girl? Save the world? Defend all that is good and smothered in rippling oil covered muscles… Easy.

Ugh, please.

No one gives a spinach injected Popeye about the hero's motives because they're all the sodding same.

But your villain… Oh, now your beautiful villain is the interesting character who sweeps in with a real serial killing reason to chew your hero's ear off and use his chest hair as dental floss. And that's what he needs to do because having a substantial motive makes the plot believable which hooks readers and drives them on to finish your book.

If your villain has no real motive, neither does your hero. Likewise, if your hero has no real motive, then neither does your villain.

It's chicken and egg. Actually, screw the chicken *and* the egg. Motives are more fundamental than even the primordial sludge, and without that prehistoric mud pie, we wouldn't be here, so motives are pretty freaking important.

Motives are story mechanics, pillars of structural necessity. Without them, you're fuckled, sideways… With a giant piranha covered pogo stick. Forget the motive, and it's not good news for your book: the only best-selling list it'll land on is Never Neverland's #DoNotFinish pile.

Got it? Good, let's move on.

Cause Really, It's All Just Yin And Yang, Init?

If your villain isn't striving for something like his blackened heart depended on it, then there's no driver or reason for the hero to fight back. And that's why a villain's motive is so important.

Let me explain. If your villain doesn't have a clear goal with a clear motive, your hero ain't got peanuts when it comes to why he's fighting back.

No motive, no conflict.
No conflict, no story.

It's two sides of the same character coin, yin and yang, black and white. It's a spectrum of balance, and your hero and villain are two ends of the same scale. Indulge me for a minute with a spot of philosophical chatter.

———

Let's call 'why'- the 'cause,' and 'motive' – 'the effect.'

Why is the cause to your villain's effect. Without it, even the tritest plot will look like an Oscar winning performance compared to your 100,000-word book flop.

But wait for just a glittery-unicorn-tail-swish-of-a-minute, because cause and effect aren't just a theory of philosophy. Oh no, it's the glorious architecture of humanity. It explains our behavior.

Cause + effect and a sprinkling of villainous action = hero reaction.

Why + motive = villain action + hero reaction.

Why Leads To Motive Which Leads To Action Which Leads To Reaction

Example: Robin Hood and The Prince of Thieves, The Movie – Robin Hood is the story of a thief, stealing from rich people and giving to the poor. In the Prince of Thieves film version, the Sheriff of Nottingham wants the crown (the why).

That leads him to mistreat the people of Sherwood (action). In turn, mistreating the residents leads Robin to step up and do something about it i.e. stealing from the rich and giving to the poor (hero's reaction).

At this point, the motive is still a bit weak. Robin's a knight in shining armor at heart and a resident of Sherwood, sure. But theft is a lot of altruistic risk and effort just to help others.

So, when the Sheriff imprisons Robin's Marian-shaped lover, it helps to up the ante and gives Robin a little more reason to fight back.

Example: Thor from the Marvel Universe - If it weren't for Odin taking abandoned baby Loki from Jothunheim and bringing him up as his own (*cause*), Loki wouldn't have felt like Odin loved Thor more than him. He wouldn't have developed an inferiority complex, and he wouldn't have needed to prove himself as a worthy son and King of Asgard (*effect*).

Loki's motive is stolen from the old school of villain storytelling. He has an inferiority complex fueling a deep need to prove himself worthy to his father. This leads him to a series of bad decisions that ultimately get him the exact opposite of what he wants.

If You're Gonna Knife A Dude In The Crown Jewels, You Gotta Have A Reason Why

We all do things for a reason.

Tattoo that phrase on your knee cap, or lip, or better, your index finger. But remember it, because it's true and right, and glorious.

Let me give you an example. The reason you avoid giving your kids sugary treats on a daily basis is because

a) Society says so, and no one needs plastic judgey-moms going all green shit and smoothies on you.

b) #RottenTeeth.

c) Because too much sugar makes you fat and unhealthy, and your kids psychotic.

In STEP 5, we examine President Snow from *The Hunger Games* in more detail. But, he's also an example of the reason why is so important.

Character Example: President Snow from the Hunger Games by Suzanne Collins – Snow does the opposite of what you'd expect a villain to do: he gets the opportunity to kill Katniss (the protagonist, his enemy) after she screws him over, and doesn't. He spares her because killing her would cause him to lose favor with his public. **He begrudgingly spares her life, BUT for a reason.**

Your villains, even the serial killing psychopaths like Freddie Kruger, have a reason for killing. *Kruger's is a desire for revenge*.

Everyone loves to hate a villain, as much as they love kicking back and relaxing after a long day at work. But readers won't hate your villain if you don't give her a decent motive.

For your average villain, her motive or reasons why should justify her actions, especially the heinous, blood covered actions.

Without proper cause for kidnapping your hero's six-year-old kid, your villain is going to be one (or all) of three things:

1. **A cliché**
2. **Have no depth**
3. **Unbelievable**

Either way, she will not achieve her black belt in villainy.

But don't get me wrong, you don't need to have pages and pages of motives/why explanation either.

Example: Captain Hook character from Peter Pan by J.M. Barrie – Hook's motive is his hatred of Peter. But the reason why he hates him is that Peter cut his hand off giving him his iconic 'hook.'

Example: Snow White and the Seven Dwarfs – The Evil Queen in *Snow White* is driven by vanity and a deep-seated need to be the most beautiful woman alive (her why). Her motive to attack Snow comes when Snow's beauty threatens her position as the 'most beautiful.'

Motive = conflict

Motive drives conflict.

Motives give a character a reason for doing something. That character then carries out 'that something' – usually an action which results in conflict.

If you don't have a motive, your characters still do things in your story. Your villain still attacks your hero. But

the reader doesn't believe or understand why she attacked the unsuspecting hero.

When your villain's gut punching your hero, your reader asks why? Saying, "Well, umm, cause she doesn't like him," is the equivalent of a limp fish act during 'husband and wife' time. It's perfunctory, unconvincing and totally vanilla. Nobody likes a vanilla villain.

Apples And Pears Like Motives and Goals

You know why is important because it drives bad guys, generates motives and drills into the coalish sludge of a villain's black heart. But goals are different. They don't drive behavior. **Goals are outcomes, real sticky hold-in-your-hands 'things' a villain wants to do, or achieve or destroy.**

Goals are the 'what' of a villain's plan. Want to break into a bank and steal a gazillion dollars? Want to kill the protagonist in a Chinese water torture festival of death? Those are your villain's goals.

The goal is the what a villain wants. The motive is the reason why he wants it.

And to be a fully rounded villain, he needs both a motive and a goal.

Ask yourself:

- What is the villain striving for?
- Why is it so important to her?
- How and when does whatever she's striving for, get in the way of the hero's goal?
- What obstacles might she need to put in the hero's way?

- Does she have a plan to reach her goal?
- Will she need to double cross the hero to reach her goal?
- Does she need or have any help from others like henchmen?

Example: Alien, The Movie - Take the cult classic film *Alien*. Set in space, an alien species finds its way on board Ripley's (the protagonist's) ship. A cat and mouse game of kill or be killed ensues all the way back to Earth.

Although it looks like a classic action fest of explosions and flamethrowers because most of the film is spent with the alien and Ripley trying to kill each other, there are actually motives and goals behind the action.

The alien is trying to reproduce and needs human bodies to do so (goal); its motive is survival.

So even in films that appear to be pure action, with non-humanoid creatures for villains, the screenwriters still create the baddies with motives and goals.

Mr. Villain Doesn't Share Goals

A lot of heroes and villains have opposing goals, but you can break the mold.

In fact, some amazing stories do the exact opposite. Like Thor and Loki, from the Marvel movies, they even have the same motive.

Example: Thor and Loki from the Marvel Universe - Loki and Thor are examples of a hero and a villain (technically Loki is an anti-hero, but more on that later). Both are striving for the same goal and in this instance, with the same motives. They both want the Asgard throne, and both want to prove themselves worthy as King to their father, Odin. However, their whys for wanting the throne are different.

Loki wants the throne to prove himself worthy because he discovers he's not Odin's blood son and has an inferiority complex. Thor wants to prove himself worthy because Odin takes him down a peg or two by showing him to be an unworthy leader.

Thor wants to be king for his people. Loki wants to be king for himself.

STEP 3 - Motivating Your Goals Summary

- The word why is the source of everything. It gives us our purpose, motivations, and goals.

- If your villain has no real motive, neither does your hero. Likewise, if your hero has no real motive, then neither does your villain.

- If your villain isn't striving for something like his life depends on it, there's no reason for the hero to fight back. And that's why a villain's motive is so important.

- No motive, no conflict. No conflict, no story.

- Cause + effect and a sprinkling of villainous action = hero reaction.

- Most heroes and villains will have opposing goals, but they don't have to.

- We all do things for a reason. Even serial killing villains like Freddie Kruger.

- Goals are outcomes, real sticky hold-in-your-hands 'things' a villain wants to do, or achieve or destroy.

- The goal is the what a villain wants. The motive is the reason why he wants it. To be a fully rounded villain, he needs both a motive and a goal.

- Without proper cause your villain is going to be one of three things:

1. A cliché
2. Have no depth
3. Be unbelievable

- Motive drives conflict.

Questions To Think About

Thinking about the genre you write, can you think of an example where the hero and villain share the same goals and motives?

Write a list of as many motives as you can.

STEP 4 - Psych Major In A Villain's History

It's All Science And History

I talked about hero worship earlier. We writers can't help but drool over our protagonists. We create rich and full histories for our heroes because we know it leads to character depth. But for some mysterious reason, we ignore the villain. Why? We need to stop that, immediately.

Character depth doesn't always mean spewing the messy backstory-innards of a character all over the page. In fact, you don't have to include backstory explicitly in your novel if you **know the source and cause of a character's behavior because it enables you to give his reactions to each plot situation more depth.**

Character interviews are nice if you want to capture backstory for your hero or minor characters. But villains need something more, something deeper because asking which shade of candy pink lip fluff your she-devil prefers is only so helpful if you need to get to the core of her psyche.

Life VS Fiction

Humans are a culmination of roughly 30,000 days of life. That's 720,000 hours of experiences and a boat load of love, heartbreak, loss and success. We are a product of our experiences in the same way a newborn baby is the fruit of a jolly good seeing to and nine months of hard bun-in-the-oven growing graft.

Our history makes us who we are: remember the day you gave an old lady your umbrella? A handsome man saw you do it and decided to walk you all the way to work under his umbrella, so you didn't get wet. You married that man. Okay, maybe that didn't exactly happen, but I bet you can think of something similar that did. The point is, we're all products of our experiences.

I hate putting people in boxes, and I know there's a nature-nurture debate, but **this is fiction,** so get over it and put stuff in boxes. Character creation is a juxtaposition because often getting depth, something you'd think requires complexity, actually requires simplicity. For example, if you grow up to be strong and confident, the likelihood is, you had one of two upbringings:

1. A happy childhood with love and cuddles and support that molded you into a confident adult.

2. Or a horrible, lonely childhood having to fend for yourself, but instead of falling the wrong side of the line you said 'f**k you life' and fought back, growing up to be strong, confident and independent.

Character Example: Michael Oher from The Movie Blind Side - based on a true story, Oher's mom was a drug addict, so he had to fend for himself from a young age, and was regularly homeless, among other atrocities. A wealthy mom notices him late at night on the street and takes him home. After a rocky start, the family adopts him, and he becomes an international American football star.

Soul Scars Make Us Or Break Us

I might be cruddy at math, but I am a huge lover of logic. Which is why I know that:

The things that shape us most in life are the experiences that have the biggest impact.

Everybody has that one person that got away and broke their heart. The one that even after thirty years have passed, and the curve of their face has blurred, the way they touched your skin, and the quiver they created in your heart has never faded. These are the experiences that make us or break us. They sculpt the shape of our souls and change the way our brains process information. Maybe you survived a car crash, saved someone's life, or lost a limb during a war, or maybe you never made it to your father's deathbed. I think of these experiences as **soul scars**. I've collated a short list of soul scars in the appendix for you to ponder and use.

We all have soul scars, even villains. Whatever your soul scar(s) are, they mark you as a person. These marks are often the source of a villain's motive and his why.

The Difference Between A Hero And A Villain

What is it that sets a villain apart from a hero? How do a pair of identical twins, brought up in the same environment, end up in opposite positions? I mentioned Cal and Maven half-brothers from the Red Queen earlier. Cal is a hero and Maven a villain. Thor and Loki are another example.

I'm a **control freak**. I ought to wear a badge that brandishes the fact as a warning. One thing we control freaks hate is that we can't always control what happens to us. It's a bitch, but it's true. But in true life-philosophy style, what we **can** control are our reactions to those situations. And it's those reactions a villain messes up.

Although experiences and soul scars shape a person, it's how a person reacts to them that define who they are and what they become.

Everything in life comes down to choice. We choose how we react to situations. We can opt to give up and accept our fate, or we can stand and fight back.

It's these choices that lead one brother to heroism and the other into villainy. Sure, a villain can be subject to shitty experiences, but you know what? So can a hero. It's the villain's choice to let it define him as a victim and send him down a reckless path. We choose to make ourselves victims; it's our decision to play with cotton candy and fairy dust, or earwigs and rotting carcasses.

Everything comes down to choice. Your villain's reactions to their soul scar experiences define him and lead him to villainy.

What separates a villain from a hero are the decisions and choices he makes.

Being 'good' and 'moral' is hard work, often painful and usually involves a lot of self-sacrifices which means it's never the easy option. And that's why villains tend to opt for the easy road because well, it's easier and gives them what they want faster than doing it the right way. But that option just gives them a one-way ticket to the villain funfair of doom.

Complexing The Psyche

Unless your villain is emotionally weak - then generally, it is the repeated, long-term or sustained experience of soul scars that leads them to wander down the path of evil. Not one off experiences.

For example, failing at something once, say an exam, is tough, but if we're honest, unless we're Einstein, we've all failed at something in life. I failed my driving test... Twice! It's a life lesson and something we all should experience at least once. But when you fail the same exam five times, or repeatedly fail a string of tests, that leaves a different kind of mark. In popular psychology, it can form what's known as a psychological complex.

In the case of exam failure, a person might feel stupid, worthless or incapable. That feeling sustained over a period and drilled home through multiple failures changes a person's mindset forming a complex.

N.B. Not everyone that fails exams repeatedly (or fails anything repeatedly for that matter), forms a complex. This is an examination of how a villain's psyche could form, not a statement of fact or something to be generalized to everyone.

A complex is a pattern of experiences (emotional, physical, etc). that form in a person's unconscious mind and influences future behaviors, attitudes and thoughts.

Exams are a form of judgment. Failing to measure up to someone's (the exam's) judgment can give the complex a burning desire to prove itself successful to counteract the negativity of failing. But it wants to prove itself *in ways other than how it originally failed to protect itself from repeating the original failure.* This is important. Unconsciously, a person's complex knows it can't succeed at the thing it's been failing at, so it overcompensates by trying to succeed at other things that are closely (or sometimes completely unrelated). For example:

- Cheating in an exam
- Finding other types of exams/tests like sports races or competitions to win
- Overachieving in other subjects

A villain with a complex often doesn't accept responsibility for his failings which leads to a desire to 'beat' others. Like those who have done better than him. In fiction, that's usually the hero. **The need to beat the hero validates his complex-driver, which is to prove he is 'successful' and not a 'failure.'** In this instance, the need to 'succeed' is overtaken by the desire to beat the hero in an exam and so the hero becomes the villain's nemesis and conflict is formed.

The need to validate the complex (and annihilate the hero) is overwhelming for the villain. It consumes him until he will do anything (at any cost) to win and beat the hero. Unfortunately for the villain, this leads him to make really stupid-bad decisions. This is the point of no return.

But what is a bad decision and what kind of bad decisions do villains make? And what is the difference between a hero's bad decision and a villain's?

Character Example: Scar character from The Lion King, The Movie - Scar is the younger brother of the Lion King, Mufasa. Scar wants the crown and makes a series of bad decisions trying to get it. The most significant of which gets him killed.

Bad decision 1: Scar tricks Prince Simba (the protagonist, Mufasa's son and Scar's nephew) to risk his life.
Bad decision 2: Instead of saving his brother, Scar kills Mufasa.
Bad decision 3: Scar tricks Simba into leaving the pride lands after his father's death.

But the two decisions that lead to his death are: allowing a pack of hyenas (which ultimately kill him) into the pride lands and underestimating Simba and his friends. The latter of which is a common mistake for villains.

Justify A Villain's Motive - Find The Source Of Your Villain's Complex

Finding the source of your villain's complex is, well, complex! There are as many sources and root causes for a complex as there are villains.

Soul scars are one cause especially if they are a negative scar. For example, failing or being bullied or being abused or being adopted like Dr. Evil from *Austin Powers*, or the lack of adoption like Lord Voldemort from the *Harry Potter* series.

You can also use a villain's positive soul scars to create a complex too. For example, if the only person that ever loved your villain was his mother (the positive part), and he is rejected constantly by potential girlfriends, thus failing to find a woman to fall *in* love with him, that too could develop a complex. He'd believe the lie that he is unworthy of 'real' sexual love. There are tons of examples of villains with mommy complexes like Smee in *Peter Pan* or Dolokhov from *War and Peace*.

Take the cause: a soul scar– and build layer upon layer of reaffirming experiences. Fear of rejection? Have the villain rejected countless times. Fear of being unloved? Then make your villain feel unloved, *repeatedly*.

The magic happens when you bring in your hero. Your hero needs to get (whether purposefully taking it, or by accident) the one thing your villain wants.

Character Example: Tom Riddle (Lord Voldemort) from The Harry Potter Series by J.K. Rowling – Tom Riddle was unloved, orphaned and never adopted. In a glorious bout of karmic literary synchronicity, Harry got what Voldemort wanted; he was loved so much by his parents they made the ultimate sacrifice for him. A sacrifice that caused Voldemort's temporary death, something that rubbed salt in Voldemort's orphan wound.

A hero almost always takes away what the villain wants, and sometimes, they use it to defeat him too.

Everybody Needs An Arc, Even The Arch Nemesis

There's a misperception that the only character that needs a character arc is the hero, but that just isn't true folks; it's as disturbing as finding a spider's leg in a half-eaten bar of chocolate. Every character in your novel goes on a journey through your plot. I'm not suggesting every sub character, and one-page cameo needs a full-blown arc but some, like your villain, do.

The easiest and simplest way to differentiate between your hero and your villain's arc is as reversals of each other.

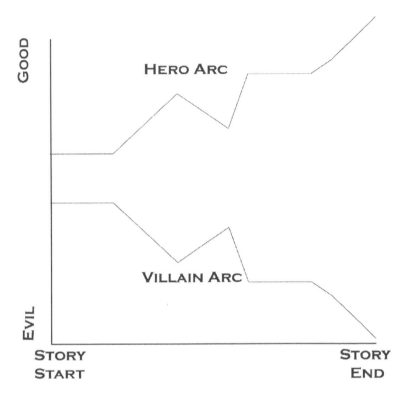

Don't take the graph literally. It's not suggestive of a 'perfect' arc; it's a hypothetical example. Your characters' arcs need to fit your story and timeline which mean the kinks and bumps in the graph above will look different to your story.

The chart shows that where your hero is in an upwards arc, your villain is in a downward one.

A character arc is an inner journey a character goes on during your plot. The arc represents the change in your character, where they begin your story as one person and

end it having grown and developed into a different version of themselves as a result of the experiences in your novel.

Why Should I Care About A Villain's Arc Anyway?

A character arc gives your story pace, conflict, and beautifully mangled plot roots. More importantly, a villain's arc creates a sense of depth.

Unless you write crime and you have a serial killer, or an 'evil from the start' type villain then your bad guy is probably going to grow into his evil role. His traits will be negative from the start but hopefully with a sprinkling of positivity. His desire to 'win' or 'beat' the hero will increase as your plot progresses and favors the hero.

The hero and villain's arcs are usually directly proportionate to each other. **As the hero begins to succeed, the villain makes increasingly bad decisions to try and beat (or suppress) the growing hero.**

Arcs also help readers sympathize with your villain because they follow him on his journey from the start, which means readers see a shred of humanity and then watch his demise as a consequence of bad timing, poor decisions, and shitty luck. Likewise, having a functional character arc makes your readers grow to love your hero, just like the last spoon of ice cream is so much tastier than the first.

`Character Example: Scar character from` `The Lion King, The Movie -` Scar from the Lion King grows bitter as Simba wins the pride's favor.

The more Mufasa defends Simba and runs to
his aid, the worse Scar's jealousy gets
and the deeper his hatred goes.

When Simba returns as an adult lion, with
confidence and strength, Scar makes
increasingly bad decisions until the
balance is tipped and Simba throws Scar
over a cliff to his death.

The Big Bad Wolf's Lie - Breaking Down A Villain's Arc

But what is a villain's arc?

We've already discussed that people (including villains) do
things for a reason unless they're just plain insane. But that's
especially true of atrocious acts. If a villain commits the murder
of an innocent person, it will be because they believe it's the
right thing to do, or if not for the right reason then because they
believe they are justified in doing it.

But how does a villain get to the point where they believe
something so wrong, could be so right?

Often the source of these beliefs are lies. **Their lives (and
more often than not, their complexes) have led them to
believe a lie.** And they don't just believe the lie; they've become
incarcerated into it. Like bloodhounds wired to sniff out deer,
villains believe their lie so fervently they'll pursue it no matter
the cost and all so they can disprove the negative belief the lie
has created.

But a villain's lie is never proved wrong. When a lie is
confirmed, it leaves a villain with nothing, meaning they have

nothing to lose either. Usually, this is shortly before your story's climax.

Heroes always have something to lose. It keeps them caring and fighting.

Villains, once their lie is confirmed, have nothing to lose and that makes them dangerous.

Example: Thor's Lie, the character from The Marvel Universe – Thor believes that he is the rightful leader and heir to Asgard because he is the son of Odin. He thinks that means he should inherit his reign over Asgard, no questions asked.

But during the story, Odin places a spell on Thor's Mjolnir hammer because he wants to teach him a lesson. The spell he casts only lets those worthy of the hammer's power use it.

Thor's lie (**that he is worthy no matter what because of his blood**) is nullified when he storms his way into S.H.I.E.L.D's building to retrieve his hammer and can't lift it.

He discovers the enchantment and realizes that until he can prove he is worthy, it's game over on hammer time. Thor learns that power and leadership have to be earned and through a lot of self-sacrifices, putting his people first and pushing his planet-sized ego aside.

Eventually, he proves himself worthy, retrieves the hammer and invalidates the lie he believed.

Example: *Loki's lie, the character from The Marvel Universe* - In the same movie, Loki grows up jealous of Thor because he thinks Odin favors him.

In Loki's mind, **he believes he is the inferior son.** This lie is reiterated when Thor starts his coronation ceremony to become king, affirming the lie that Loki is neither a worthy son nor a worthy king.

The final proof Loki needs to confirm this lie comes when he discovers that Odin took him from Jotunheim during the war between Asgard and the frost giants. Odin reveals he is not Loki's birth father and then falls into a deep, long-lasting sleep.

Loki then makes a series of bad decisions trying to prove his worth as king and son. When Odin finally wakes up, he disapproves of everything Loki has done.

This is the final nail in Loki's lie coffin. He now resolutely believes and accepts the lie (that he is unworthy) is true. He's lost everything that means something to him: the crown, his father, and his family. At the end of the film, Loki falls to his apparent death, but the last scene in the film shows him having returned, and the audience knows he now has nothing to lose and a pretty big vendetta against Thor.

In Summary:

- Loki's complex forms the basis of the lie he believes which he developed from his soul scar - being adopted.
- He has an inferiority complex, spawned from the continued presumption that Thor is the preferred son and Thor's constant bettering of him.
- This leads Loki to believe he is unworthy of being Odin's son and of being King of Asgard.
- The inferiority complex causes him to make bad decisions, like tricking Thor into remaining banished on Earth.
- And that results in Odin disapproving of Loki's behavior, supporting Thor, and affirming the lie that he is not worthy.

The difference between a hero's lie and a villain's is that heroes have theirs invalidated. Whereas villains have them affirmed.

The lie is one of the most significant plot devices you can use to drive a hero's arc, and it's the same for a villain.

Put It All Together, And You Get Cake? No, Wait. I Mean A Villain

The reason a lie works to mold an arc is that it allows your characters to realize a truth: they learn something new that develops their inner self during your plot.

I hate oversimplifications because nothing's really ever as simple as it's made out to be, especially villains because there are a million and one options to create their delicious nuances. But, and here's where I contradict myself because you can boil down arcs, depth, and lies into one beautifully oversimplified equation. If you add this chapter up, you get a villainous formula.

Soul scars + NEGATIVE TRAITS = COMPLEXES which create the LIE your villain BELIEVES which leads to BAD DECISIONS.

Questions To Help You Find The Source Of A Villain's Complex

Rather than understanding the ins and outs of your character's favorite hobbies, colors, brand of smokes or fluffy pet bunny's name, ask yourself the deep and meaningful questions. Pick up your therapist clipboard and lie back on the chaise lounge. Probe your character's darkest, stickiest, nastiest corners and get to the core of their emotions, values and thought patterns.

For example, ask yourself:

- What or who would they die for?
- What does love feel like to them?
- Have they ever been in love?
- Are they capable of loving someone or something?
- What does success look like to them?
- What are their positive soul scars?
- What are their negative soul scars?
- What's their worst memory?
- What's their happiest memory?
- Are they afraid of anything?

- What's their deepest desire?
- What are their negative traits?
- What are their positive traits?
- What's their greatest achievement?
- Have they ever sacrificed their desires for someone else?
- What are the most significant events in their lives?
- Are they proud of anything?
- Are they ashamed of anything?
- What's the worst thing they've ever done?
- What's their relationship like with their parents?
- What was their childhood like?
- Do they have any misperceptions about the world?
- What lie do they believe?

STEP 4 - Psych Major In A Villain's History Summary

- Understanding the source and cause of a character's behavior enables you to give them and their reactions to each plot situation more depth.

- The things that shape us the most in life are the experiences that have the biggest impact.

- Soul scars are the experiences in our life that are so fundamental they change us for the better and sometimes for the worse. These soul scars influence us, our behaviors, thoughts, decision making, and actions.

- Soul scars are a great source for developing a villain's motive and his why.

- Everything comes down to choice. Although experiences and soul scars shape a person, it's how a person reacts to them that defines who they are and what they become. What separates a villain from a hero is the decisions they make.

- Unless your villain is emotionally weak - then generally, it is the repeated, long-term or sustained experience of soul scars that leads them to develop a complex. Not one off experiences.

- A complex is a pattern of experiences (emotional, physical, etc). that form in a person's unconscious mind and influence future behaviors, attitudes and thoughts. It is also a protective mechanism that works unconsciously to counteract the negative emotions a person has formed about themselves. Its purpose is to move a person from a negative mindset to a positive one. This is why it influences decision making and leads a villain to make bad choices.

- Complexes need to prove the lie a person believes wrong and do so in a way that is different to how the lie was created.

- Your hero needs to get the one thing your villain wants.

- The easiest and simplest way to differentiate between your hero and your villain's arc is as reversals of each other.

- A character arc is an inner journey a character goes on during your plot.

- Heroes have something to lose. It keeps them caring and fighting.

- Villains, once their lie is confirmed, have nothing to lose and that makes them dangerous to your hero.

- The difference between a hero's lie and a villain's is that a hero has her lie invalidated, whereas a villain has his affirmed.

- **Soul scars + NEGATIVE TRAITS = COMPLEXES which = THE LIE YOUR VILLAIN BELIEVES which lead to BAD DECISIONS.**

Questions To Think About

Looking at the list of soul scars in the appendix, what other scars or experiences can you think of that would leave such a considerable mark on someone's life?

Think about the villains in your genre. What types of complexes can you identify?

STEP 5 - Credibility + Believability = Authentic Villain

I first watched *The Exorcist* when I was nine; I'm not sure whether it was the fountain of projectile vomit or badly done makeup, but I wasn't impressed. Even as a wee snot-nosed kiddie I had my skeptical eyebrow set to 'firmly risen.' I was too cool for school, and nothing would scare me because I was 'invincible', and clearly, I was also an arrogant prick.

These days it's a little different because I know some things go bump in the night. Scary movies, books, and stories have a bigger impact on me because my imagination is that bit sharper. After watching something scary, I tend to leave the lights on, scan rooms and ceilings and ensure there's a hockey stick or preferably medieval flail within reaching distance.

But that's horror. And this book is not about horror. It's about villains, and you don't need to write horror to create a scary villain. But you do need to chisel out the villainous building blocks to create credibility and believability.

Without those two elements, you can toss any scare-factor you want to create into the trash because your readers will be reduced to versions of my cocky nine-year-old self. Only they have the ability to leave you a condescending review in a very public arena.

But what makes a villain credible?

What Is Credibility?

If you check a dictionary, it will talk about **being believable and creating trust.**

If you flicked back to believability, it would say something along the lines of having confidence in the reliability of something without proof.

Those are strong sentences and bold words that without the right tools, might make your average writer retreat into the safety of a firmly replaced pen lid.

But fear not, it's just a simple equation.

Credibility + believability = authentic villain.

Core Like An Apple, Only Grab The Seeds And Toss The Rest

Credibility, like in real life, is built, and values are one of the building blocks.

You might think that heroes are the only ones that need values but if you do, you're wrong. So, don't think that. Okay, let's move on.

A value is something that has some worth or importance.

I don't mean sentimental value like the trinket box of Granddad Bill's taxidermy insect collection that Granny Doris clings to because it's the only thing she has left of him. **I'm talking personal values. The inner philosophical truths we abide by and believe until our dying breath.**

For example, being good to others; staying loyal no matter the cost; helping old ladies cross the road. If I did a post mortem on you, what would I find wriggling around your diaphragmatic core?

Having values is seen as a positive thing because, well, *it is* positive. It separates out your Prince Charming, perfectly ironed, crimped, primped and starched white shirt wearing Clark Kent from your filthy-dirty street criminal-like Lucifer.

But because of the stereotyped assumption, that values = good, we word artists often leave values out of a villain's repertoire, resulting in the loss of character depth.

Which is very wrong too.

Because everyone has values, even villains.

The Two Vs – Villains And Values

There are two ways values can be incorporated into a villain's character.

1. Having a positive value, they enact in a bad way

2. Having a negative value

Let's take the first - a positive value enacted in a bad way.

Villains are notorious for placing a high value on loyalty. But it's the actions a villain takes when someone breaks their value (i.e. breaks their loyalty), that shows their true nature, bringing them squarely back into the villain arena, giving their character that extra little sizzle.

Character Example: Lord Voldemort from the Harry Potter series by J.K. Rowling – Lord Voldemort is a classic example of a villain who places a high value on loyalty. So much so, he brands his followers with the Dark Mark and kills anyone who changes their mind and wants out.

Character Example: Hannibal Lecter from Silence of the Lambs by Thomas Harris – Hannibal Lecter places a high value on manners and gets real pissed when another prisoner throws semen in Clarice's face. In fact, that's what makes him engage with Clarice's case and what causes him to offer her help. That infringement of his values drives the plot forward.

Everyone has values, even villains. But it's how a character reacts when those values are broken that define whether they're a hero or villain.

The one exception to that rule is the category of villains, the often psychotic and deranged ones, whose values are pure evil, like Michael Myers from the *Halloween* films or Patrick Bateman from *American Psycho* written by Bret Easton Ellis.

Myers is a psychopath and murders for the sake of enjoyment, and he places a high value on fulfilling his desires. Bateman kills out of anger and frustration. But not all serial killer characters are the same.

Character Example: Freddie Kruger from A Nightmare on Elm Street - Freddie bucks the trend because he values revenge. Freddie is a child murderer who gets released on a technicality. The kid's angry parents team up and chase Krueger into a building. They burn it down while he's trapped inside, giving Krueger his

burnt facial appearance and his
subsequent thirst for revenge.

Krueger's credible because his revenge-
value is both credible and realistic. If
someone irrevocably burns your face,
you're not going to be happy about it,
and rightly or wrongly, you're probably
going to want revenge.

Core Values

In the appendices, I've included a list of core values for
you to rummage through. Once you give your villain a value,
they need to stick to it like glue because **values, like traits,
produce consistent behaviors in your characters.**

Think of the annoyingly heroic fairy tale knight in shining
armor. His constant save the day actions represent the value
he places on both lives and being a gentleman. Valuing life
+ manners = a consistent behavior *(saving dames)*.

Believe To The Death

Values are the most important non-materialistic thing we
have. They are part of who we are; they help to define us
because they are beliefs. When you believe something that
strongly it becomes a part of who you are, which is why
you'll fight to the death over it. That's why someone
breaking your values results in such a severe consequence.

A Hero's Values VS A Villain's Values - The Hunger Games

Character Example: Katniss Everdeen hero from The Hunger Games by Suzanne Collins - Katniss Everdeen values family over everything. For Katniss, her sister is her life. She would (and does) sacrifice everything to protect her. Katniss volunteers to take her sister's place during the Reaping (an event where the government comes to collect a child from each district to fight to the death, and only one child survives). She values family so highly she would die for them.

Example: President Coriolanus Snow villain character from The Hunger Games by Suzanne Collins - Snow is President of an autocratic system in the country of Panem. He believes in his system of regulation, hierarchy, and segregation. He's particularly strict on enforcing the reality TV game show (The Hunger Games).

The show masquerades as a peacekeeping competition to keep the peace between the districts and prevent an uprising or repeat of the dark days when the districts rebelled against the Capitol and their world was at war.

His enjoyment of it calls his sanity into question as he displays psychopathic tendencies. Despite that, Snow has two values he sticks to rigidly.

- He only kills for a purpose.
- He always tells the truth.

Integral Integrity

Integrity is adhering to your moral, ethical or value based principles. A kind of moralistic honesty.

This is one of those things, like values, which gets mistaken for a hero-centric attribute. But a villain can have integrity just as much as your hero next door can.

If a bad guy sticks to his values, even if that means doing something awful, then he has integrity, and integrity breeds credibility, authenticity, and believability.

Character Example: President Coriolanus Snow villain character from The Hunger Games by Suzanne Collins - President Snow believes you should only kill for a purpose. The Hunger Games is his justified purpose.

Snow sticks to the rules of the Hunger Games (that only one child should be left standing) rigidly. Which is why when Katniss breaks the rules and makes a suicide pact with Peeta (the other remaining child in the games), it saves them both. Snow reasons there has to be someone left standing because those are the rules, so he chooses two winners over none. Despite saving both Katniss and

Peeta, Snow is furious, and Katniss becomes his mortal enemy.

Even though Snow's values are warped and wrong, they're still his values. He has integrity because he sticks to them. He refuses to kill Katniss even after her betrayal because he doesn't have a reason to.

Authenticating Evil With Gold Stars

Authenticity is brewed, like beer, from credibility and integrity. It's genuine and real and embodies humanity.

Your villain needs to be authentic because it's part and parcel of being credible and believable. Think of someone you admire, a leader at work, perhaps an author, or a leader in the scientific community. I'd be willing to bet you a month's salary they're authentic. Only the best, most authentic leaders get to the top.

Your villain is a leader. Authentic leaders do exactly what they say they will, even if it's hard or painful and that's precisely what your villain needs to do too. Especially if it means torturing your protagonist or killing off a couple of minor characters your hero happens to care about.

Example: The Hunger Games by Suzanne Collins - President Snow could have killed Katniss for disobeying him. It would have pleased him, but it wouldn't have served a purpose (which goes against his values) and would have lost him favor with the public. So, he takes the hard decision, bites his bottom lip and lets her live. That makes him real. He's human because we see how much he wants to kill her, and yet he follows through with his convictions even when it's hard.

Humanity makes a character real to a reader, even if the humanity is dark.

If you don't make your villains follow through on their values and beliefs, they'll look weak and flaky.

The Expert Villain = The Unbeatable Villain

You may think your hero is the only one that needs to be an expert at something but actually, villains should be experts in something too.

What do I mean by 'expert'? Well, what he doesn't need is a rod up his sphincter, spectacles, and a white lab coat. Experts are intelligent and brilliant at something. But what that something is, doesn't really matter. What's important is that he is better than your hero at something.

Why's that important?

Because it makes the villain hard to beat. **Villains need to be hard to beat. Otherwise, your plot won't carry enough tension related ups and downs to grip the reader to the end.**

If your villain isn't hard to beat then he's not very credible, or believable, as a bad guy able to give your hero a rough time.

Having a villain that's hard to beat also means your villain can torture your hero and prevent him from getting what he most desires. It means that your sweet, shiny, blond-locked knight is an underdog, and who doesn't love an underdog? An intelligent, expert villain will be two steps ahead of the hero. That makes them hard to beat. Especially when you take away all the hero's resources. Besides, nobody likes a hero that wins the first time, every time.

Villain-hero battles need to be extreme, dangerous and downright life-threatening, or your dear readers will fall into a boredom coma. A villain needs to appear unbeatable, for 85% of your novel. Remove all hope from your hero and his unlikely bandits, until, suddenly, a magical beacon of villain defeating badass appears so your hero can whip out his super high-flying face kick or the orb of villain doom.

Expertise constitutes anything that your villain is better at than your hero.

Everybody Has Secrets, And Everybody Tells Lies - But It Needs To Be Transparent As Glass

Putting transparency and secrets in the same sentence sounds like an epic contradiction. And in a way, it is. But also, it's not. A villain needs to have secrets and tell lies, but they also need to be super transparent about it. Like a salesman on stage or a cheerleader on a football pitch who only has eyes for one jock, except 'honest,' she's cheering for the whole team.

The reader needs to know your villain is hiding something and grip the pages with anticipation over what they've got planned for your hero. Your villain can threaten, abuse and outright blurt out their goal to your hero (there's your transparency), **but what they can't do is tell them *how* they're going to do whatever it is they have planned.** Unless of course, they plan on double crossing the hero.

There's something super sinister about a villain that can articulate their goals with absolute precision and clarity. I mean, what's scarier than someone who is crystal clear that if you cross them, they'll extract your finger nails using nothing but a pair of rusted tweezers and their strangely sharp teeth?

And this comes back to what I said earlier. **A villain has to follow through with their threats.** If the consequence of your hero not handing over a ransom fee is little Johnny getting a finger cut off, then little Johnny's fingers have got to go.

Transparency doesn't have to be as obvious as the villain shouting I am going to ax your mom to death. You can be subtle with your transparent intentions - **a tilt of the head; a squint of the eye; body language. Often what's not said and silence are more powerful literary devices than verbalizing a villain's goals.**

The illusion of secrets, through body language and silence, is just as powerful as actually having them. It creates fear in your protagonist and your reader. You need that. You need your reader desperate to turn the page to find out if crazy old Mertle is going to kill her husband's mistress or not.

Your hero needs to know your villain is coming and why (transparency) but not know how, or when (secrets).

STEP 5 - Credibility + Believability = Authentic Villain Summary

- Credibility is about being believable and creating trust.

- There's a simple equation for creating authenticity:

- Credibility + believability = authentic villain.

- A value is something that has some kind of worth or importance.

- There are two ways values can be incorporated into a villain's character:

  1. Having a positive value, they enact in a bad way
  2. Having a negative value

- Everyone has values, even villains. But it's how a character reacts when those values are broken that defines whether they're a hero or villain.

- Like traits, values produce consistent behaviors.

- Integrity is adhering to your moral, ethical or value based principles - a kind of moralistic honesty.

- If a villain sticks to their values, even if that means doing something bad, then they have integrity.

- Authenticity is brewed, like beer, from credibility and integrity. It's genuine and real, and human. Readers like characters with humanity; even when the humanity is dark, it makes a character real.

- You don't need a hundred different traits to make a character or a villain real; you just need them to conform to the values they have.

- Think of a villain as a leader. Authentic leaders do exactly what they say they will, even if it's hard or painful and that's what your villain needs to do too.

- Villains need to be hard to beat. Otherwise, your plot won't carry enough tension related ups and downs to grip the reader to the end.

- Your hero needs to know your villain's coming and why (transparency) but not know how, or when (secrets).

Questions To Think About

Thinking about the villains in your genre, write a list of credible and non-credible villains. Compare and contrast the reasons why they either are or are not credible.

How do your favorite villains react when their values are broken?

STEP 6 - Fifty Shades Of Villain - Archetypes

There are as many villains as there are books. Each one has a flavorsome cocktail of evil spice, crushed insects, and dashes of negative traits.

Now you know I hate putting people in boxes, but if we think about it **there are patterns to people's behavior, and there are patterns to villains too.**

Likewise, many writers suggest there are only so many story plots. Christopher Booker says there are as few as seven and that every story ever told can be pigeon holed into these seven plots. Vladimir Propp said there was only one! I don't know about you, but that makes me feel all kinds of uncomfortable. I mean, the implication is that we writers aren't original.

Call it ego or creative thirst, but I used to think of us writers as imaginative little squirrels tucked away in the depths of midnight making our words and characters dance across the page all shiny, and unique. But now, I find myself asking if any of us can honestly say we've come up with a story so new and original there are no traces of it anywhere.

Think about it. How many villains can you think of and how many similarities are there between them?

There are a number of villainous 'types.' These are often called archetypes. For example, the psychopathic ax-wielding nut job that wants to cut off your left earlobe using your own elbow and a toothbrush.

Villains don't always have to be people, and they don't have to be a person either. There are the obvious ones: creatures, monsters, demons and aliens. But there are an awful lot of other types of villains too. Like internal demons (often found in romance) or invisible ideological villains like the Capitol (i.e. society's rules) in the Hunger Games. There are even the bad guys that don't exist at all because they're made up in the protagonist's hallucinogenic mind. **Internal villains can be just as powerful antagonists as flesh and blood ones can.**

In fact, having inner demons to deal with, *as well as* flesh and blood villains, makes your plot even deeper, the emotion your character feels stronger and the conflict in the story richer.

But what are all the different types of villain archetype?

The Archetypes

The Omnipotent Villain

I like to see these villains as the classics. When I think of a villain, the first thing that comes to mind is an old-school power hungry, slightly crazy-eyed, occasionally demonic, but ultimately a seriously powerful villain like Sauron from *Lord of the Rings*, or Lord Voldemort from *Harry Potter*.

Often these villains are trying to gather vast armies, enormous amounts of power whether magical, governmental or anything else. They often have a second in command, an ugly runt that does their bidding and dirty work.

Typically, **these villains have weak justifications behind their motives, but they do have motives nonetheless**. Most are fueled by their egos and want more... More power, authority, servants, slaves, armies and more than anything, they want more control and power.

Often these villains are depicted as narcissistic, arrogant, egotistical, self-centered and with deep-seated self-importance.

This villain will stop at nothing to get what he wants, when he wants it and exactly how he wants it. He's organized, has plans and sub-plans, and a million minions to carry out his schemes. **Rarely does this villain get his hands dirty unless it's in the final battle or story climax and he's trying to throttle the life out of the hero.**

Examples: Moriarty from Sherlock Holmes, Sauron from *Lord of the Rings*, Lord Voldemort from *Harry Potter* or General Zod from *Superman*, President Snow from *The Hunger Games.*

Genre Examples: Often found in fantasy novels, and science fiction novels with huge sword wielding battles. They're often in dystopian fiction where there is a corrupt leader or in children's books. The characters tend to be dark lords, army generals, presidents, warlords or rogue royals.

The Arch Nemesis

The arch nemesis is the kind of villain that grows through the plot. This type of villain can often be found in series, trilogies or books where the plot unravels over more than one novel. **This is often because the villain doesn't start out bad, or at least she doesn't start out as evil as she ends up.** It's a story of growth and change for the villain as much as it is the hero.

For example, classmates in the same school year. As the plot progresses, the hero does something that hurts the classmate or wins something the villain had worked for. In essence, the hero gets whatever her classmate wanted; like the boy she fancied.

This creates conflict which causes rivalry. As the plot develops, the conflict becomes a deep-seated hatred in the villain. A festering wart that creates a bitter mindset that makes the villain think the hero has a vendetta against her, leading to rivalry and ultimately conflict; think Regina and Cady from *Mean Girls* mentioned earlier.

In some ways, this villain is the creation of the hero herself. If it weren't for her actions (either during the plot or before it), the rivalry would never begin. Typically, the nemesis has the polar opposite traits to the hero. Where the hero is beautiful, the villain is ugly. Where the hero is kind, the villain is not.

Examples: Draco Malfoy from *Harry Potter*, Regina George from *Mean Girls*, The Sheriff of Nottingham in *Robin Hood*, and Lex Luthor from *Superman*.

Genre Examples: Often found in Young Adult books typically set in high schools. This villain is also found in any story where the protagonist and antagonist have known each other for a long time, and there is a long history of rivalry between them. This plot line is relevant to most genres.

The Deranged Lunatic

These are the villains that have mental health issues. Most commonly, they are psychopaths or sociopaths. What this means is **they don't tend to have solid motivations**. There's no reason why behind their attacks, and this is scary to readers because we know that people do things for a reason. This villain is more unpredictable than the others.

Readers like to guess what's coming. But for psychopaths and sociopaths, that's not so easy. A plot with that kind of villain is unpredictable and creates suspense taking the reader on a thrill ride.

You need to create enough depth for your villain to be convincing. You can do this by **adding sufficient backstory which creates an implied 'why' behind the villain's actions.** That then allows the reader to buy into your villain.

Examples: Hannibal Lecter from *The Silence of the Lambs*, Patrick Bateman from *American Psycho*, Norman Bates from *Psycho*, Alex from *A Clockwork Orange*, The Joker from *The Dark Knight* and John Doe from *Seven*.

Genre Examples: Often found in crime and thriller books and films, as well as action adventure and mystery and occasionally in literary fiction too.

The Revenge Whore

Some villains just can't let shit go. No matter what the hero does, the villain just keeps coming. This type of villain got snubbed by the hero. Something awful happened to the villain in her past, and now she's out for revenge at any cost.

She uses her revenge and whatever happened to her in the past as justification for committing crimes.

While the revenge villain might seem similar to an arch nemesis, the difference is, this villain doesn't have to have a vendetta against the hero specifically, or at least not to start with. It could have happened prior to the plot, or the hero could just be a victim of a more global hatred from the villain. At some point the villain is connected to the hero and then the hatred intensifies as the story progresses. Usually, this is as a consequence of a series of actions on the hero's part, and revenge is the main driver for the villain.

Example: A Nightmare on Elm Street, The Movie - Freddie Krueger was wronged by a group of kids' parents in his past. He's enacting his revenge in the present and against a scapegoated group of teenagers. One of those teenagers becomes the hero.

Examples: Freddy Krueger in *A Nightmare on Elm Street*, Michael Corleone in *The Godfather*, Maleficent from *Maleficent* and Two-Face from *The Dark Knight*.

Genre Examples: Thrillers, action stories or films, anything with violence and a thinly veiled history behind the plot, and even romance although in an antagonistic form rather than a violent villain, for example, the scorned wife.

The Secret Squirrel Villain

This villain is all about betrayal, secrets, lies, and super mega awesome plot twists.

You know when you have to put a book down because a killer twist was revealed and you need a moment to pick your jaw off the floor and replace it back with your teeth? Well, this villain does that.

This guy is super fun to write because you get to mislead and misdirect the reader. Your villain gets up to mischief and mayhem while trying to keep themselves and their evil plans disguised from the hero.

This villain could be the hero's mentor or best friend or even their parent. Readers like this villain because they sense the betrayal like a wife catching a whiff of a perfume she's never worn. **Readers can feel the tension building; they know something bad is coming, but they don't know what or who the perpetrator is. It's exciting and thrilling and gives the reader literary tingles in all the right places.** This is the kind of villain that makes the reader turn page after page late into the night.

This villain is two-faced. On the outside, they're kind and friendly and have the hero's back. All the while they are harboring resentment and hatred and plotting their downfall.

Caution: misdirect yes, but sow a seed of doubt, however small, in your reader's mind, so they don't feel cheated.

Examples: Perhaps the oldest example of this villain is Judas Iscariot from the Bible. Other examples include Alex Forrest from *Fatal Attraction*, Annie Wilkes from *Misery*, Amy from *Gone Girl*, Professor Snape from *Harry Potter* although this is a plot trick double bluff and not an actual villain, but

Professor Quirrell is a good example of this from the Harry Potter series, Natalie from *Vampire Academy* and finally Chancellor Palpatine from *Star Wars Episode III: Revenge of the Sith*.

Genre Examples: This villain is regularly found across every genre.

The Invisible, Internal

In some ways, this is the ultimate villain because he is so super bad he *really is* nearly unbeatable. The protagonist has to make enormous sacrifices and go through huge developmental arcs to be able to defeat the hardest villain of them all, himself.

The hero will spend much of the story blind to his villain; his woes and troubles will seem insurmountable because no weapon, other than the hero's choice to change himself can bring this villain down.

This is the best villain to torture your hero in both emotional and psychological ways. Nobody beats themselves up as well as themselves. Look at us writers: we don't need bad reviews to gather our trusty sea rope and attach it to the ceiling; we only need to read our first draft. Or maybe that's just me.

Example: Tyler Durden* character from *Fight Club, The Movie - My favorite example of this villain is Tyler Durden from *Fight Club*. The protagonist, played by Edward Norton and called 'The Narrator,' is oblivious to the fact he is the antagonist, Tyler Durden. The Narrator doesn't establish this fact, or the reason why he is the antagonist, until the end of the film, in what is arguably one of the best plot twists ever. If you haven't seen it, you need to. Immediately. GO. WATCH IT. NOW.

Examples: Tyler Durden from *Fight Club*, the Ring that Frodo Baggins has in *Lord of the Rings*, Venom from *Spider-Man* and Mr. Hyde, from *The Strange Case of Dr.Jekyll and Mr. Hyde*.

Genre Examples: This character is wide reaching and can be found in any genre from romance to YA to fantasy.

The Slut Seductress

The female slut villain is a cliché. And is usually a tall, leggy, gorgeous, blond (or brunette for that matter), high heel wearing sexual predator.

This girl knows she's hot, and she uses it to her advantage. She's evil to her core, wears black, red and often leather or patent shoes and lashings of makeup to make even the most famous beauty pageant winners feel amateur.

This villain is rarely male (although you could argue high school jocks/hot guys like Sebastian Valmont from *Cruel Intentions* fit this archetype). This girl has morals that would make you cry: she's sly, devious, clever, and uses her sexual prowess to entrap the hero and his comrades.

Examples: Black widows like Debbie Jellinsky from *Addams Family Values*,

Catherine Tramell from *Basic Instinct*, Lady Macbeth from *Macbeth*, Nomi Malone in *Showgirls,* Poison Ivy from *Batman*, and Kathryn Merteuil from *Cruel Intentions*.

Genre Examples: Often in stories and films aimed at a younger audience, for example, the evil stepmother character, like in Cinderella or Hansel and Gretel. But this character can also be found in adult thrillers and action movies, for example, Mystique in *X-Men*.

The Jealous One

The jealous one is usually, although not always, a sibling or family relation. You can often find examples in high school stories and films. But anywhere where there are two related characters.

This villain tends to have an inferiority complex and feelings of inadequacy which are reinforced by years of exposure to their sibling beating them, being the preferred child or having a high level of success or adoration from others, which the villain can't get.

Because of the connection between them, jealousy is often the driver behind their conflict, and it's particularly intense because it developed over a period of time, although with Loki and Thor from the Marvel Universe, the jealously is implied and not overtly stated.

Examples: The ugly stepsisters in *Cinderella*, Loki - Thor's adopted brother from *Thor* and Scar - Mufasa's younger brother from *The Lion King*.

Genre Examples: Again, this type of villain can come from any genre but is often seen in fiction or films aimed at a younger audience.

The Female Villain

This section is a difficult one to write because my intention is not to offend or irritate but, to do the topic justice, I am going to have to address some stereotypes.

Women, when described by society, are rarely portrayed as scary. Maybe, it's because *some* of us are mothers, so our gender represents motherhood. Or perhaps it's nothing to do with motherhood but the excess of estrogen, or maybe it's because we are (generally) smaller framed and not as physically strong as (most) men. Therefore, it's harder for a woman to epitomize the brutality of a killer.

I mean, there *are* plenty of real-life female criminals, although granted, fewer women are convicted of extreme crimes than men. But still; whatever the reason for society's view, it's created a misnomer that women don't make good female villains. Well, sorry, but I beg to differ!

Think of the top three villains you've come across. Got them? Good. Hold on to them for a second. Most people, if you ask them to list great villains will name characters like Hannibal Lecter, Darth Vader, Patrick Bateman and The Joker, all of which are male.

One of the reasons I wrote this book was because I wanted to write a story with a female villain. But when I researched examples in popular media, literature and TV shows, I struggled to find more than a handful of good examples.

The list that came *off the top of my head* included:

- Cruella De Vil from *101 Dalmatians*
- Ursula from *The Little Mermaid*
- One of my personal favorites, Professor Umbridge from *Harry Potter*
- Annie Wilkes from *Misery*
- Nurse Ratched from *One Flew Over the Cuckoo's Nest*
- Miranda Priestly from *The Devil Wears Prada*
- Alex Forrest from *Fatal Attraction*

That's it. Seven villains. SEVEN! Sure, there are other female baddies out there, but I couldn't think of them off the top of my head, which means they might not be mainstream enough to spring to mind like the first four male villains I mentioned.

Even if you look at well-known lists like the American Film Institute's list of the best villains and heroes, there's still only a handful of female villains on it.

Worse, **a lot of the famous female villains border on a cliché because they're written as psychotic, evil lunatics with no semblance of rational thought OR they're all given the same mental health disorder.**

I talk more about borderline personality disorder (BPD) in STEP 10, but a lot of the villains that are both famous and female are portrayed as having this disorder. For example, Eileen Wuornos from *Monster* (who is also a real-life criminal that did have BPD), Alex Forrest in *Fatal Attraction* and Nurse Ratched in *One Flew Over the Cuckoo's Nest*.

The reason female villains are often portrayed as having BPD is that it's more common for the female gender. It's the equivalent of psychopathy and sociopathy which is found more commonly in men. But that means writers need to be careful of resorting to those classic disorders because automatically giving your female villain BPD, unless it suits the story, is lazy, and as clichéd as a witch's wart.

I'm not saying you can't use BPD ever. Clearly, it's frequently used for a reason. But don't be a slacker that uses a cliché, be original.

I've been asked many times how you create credible and believable female villains. I did wonder if I was missing some Pandora's box filled with sparkly villainish wands that could cast a magic estrogen spell and give you the perfect female antagonist. But there isn't a box, and there isn't a panacea.

Because you don't have to do anything different when crafting a female villain than a male one.

The misnomer comes from the fact there aren't as many female villains in popular culture. Writers get scared, and think there's some big, bad, scary magic trick they haven't been told that pulls the perfect female villain out of a magician's hat. But that's rubbish. Bums and boobs mean nothing. If you want to create a credible female villain follow the same steps as you would for a male one. But specifically:

Credibility

Female villains don't have much of a reputation in the book market; there are less of them, which is both a problem and an opportunity.

Having a female villain gives you as a writer the opportunity to be original because there are fewer well-known she-monsters in the market to compete with. But it also means it's even more important to craft a character with skyscraper levels of credibility.

Credibility creates believability which means better female villains.

Core Values

All villains need core values, especially female villains. It makes it easier for readers to swallow a villain with a really strong core value. Values create humanity, even if those values are terrible.

Have a mix of good values and bad ones, and it's the reaction your villain has to those values being broken that makes the difference between a hero and a villain.

The values can be honorable or insane, but her reaction to a violation of them should be severe. She needs to stick to them like industrial strength super glue because it will make her character and behaviors consistent – and that creates believability. It also means your female villain has a reason to fight – values are integral to our very being, and we defend them to the death.

Integrity

Integrity means doing the right things for the right reasons such as defending what you believe in, like your values, even if they are evil.

A villain fighting with integrity thinks that what she is doing is right, for the right reasons. Even if she's doing something utterly random like some warped serial killing ladybird genocide. A writer can make it more terrifying if the villain thinks what she's doing is right.

Authenticity

Your villain needs to do exactly what she says she's going to do. Especially if that means torturing your main character or killing off someone he loves.

Without following through on her convictions, she's weak and flaky, another cliché for a female villain, but worse – it makes them beatable. Your villain needs to appear unbeatable right up until your book's climax.

Expertise

Having an intelligent villain with expertise in a particular area makes them much harder to beat, which builds the conflict and plot tension.

Make your female villain an expert in something other than parenting. Maybe she's a structural engineer, or the vice chancellor of a university, or sod it, the President of the United States.

Believability

Believability can come from playing on truth and fear. Some of the scariest things in life are those that are the closest to reality, the ones that could almost be true.

A mother who lost her child, as well as everything else, makes it easy to understand why she's been driven to insanity, to murder…to villainy. But being a mother isn't the only thing a woman does. We are more than the children we produce. We love and feel, strive and have hopes, and dreams and aspirations. So, don't lean on the 'parent' factor for your female villain's motive. Torture her with **all** of her history. Make it intricate and detailed enough that her motives are believable and credible.

Step 6 - Fifty Shades of Villain - Archetypes Summary

- There are patterns to people's behavior, and there are patterns to a villain's too.

- There are a number of villainous categories. Some like to think of them as archetypes.

- Villains don't always have to be people, they don't have to be evil, and they don't even have to be a person at all.

- Internal villains can be just as powerful as flesh and blood ones can.

- Types of Villains:

    - Omnipotent power hungry dark lord
    - The arch nemesis
    - The deranged lunatic
    - The revenge whore
    - The secret squirrel
    - The invisible internal villain
    - The slut seductress
    - The jealous one

- When people think of villains, the list is often dominated by males. While there are good examples of female villains out there, there are fewer mainstream famous ones.

- Many female villains are borderline cliché because they're written as psychotic, evil lunatics with no semblance of rational thought and often have BPD.

- You don't have to do anything different when crafting a female villain than when crafting a male one:

- **Credibility** – credibility creates believability which means better female villains.

- **Core Values** – have a mix of good values and bad ones, and it's the consequence of those values being broken that makes the difference between a hero and a villain.

- **Integrity** – integrity means doing the right things for the right reasons like defending what you believe in. For example, your values, even if they are evil.

- **Authenticity** – your villain needs to do exactly what they say they are going to do. Especially if that means torturing your main character or killing off someone they love.

- **Expertise** – having an intelligent villain with expertise in a particular area makes them much harder to beat, which builds the conflict and plot tension.

- **Believability** – can come from playing on truth and fear. I always think some of the scariest things in life are those that are the closest to reality, the ones that could almost be true.

Questions To Think About

Think about your genre. Pick your top ten favorite books. Are the villains similar? Do you find the same archetypes or are they all different?

What female villains can you think of? Are they clichéd? If they aren't, what lessons can you learn from how they're constructed?

STEP 7 - All About Anti-Heroes

Anti-Schmanti What Now?

No really, what in the name of all that is evil and villain-like, is an anti-hero? Aren't villains all villainy and heroes all, you know, heroey?

Well, yes, except also, no. There are also cheeky little characters called anti-heroes, and they happen to be my absolute favorite characters.

Anti-heroes are, in my humblest opinion, the cherry on your finger-licking villain pie. **They're two parts hero to one part villain.** Anti-heroes let you have your cake *and* eat it. She is the bacon in your BLT and the diamond in your ring.

Cough Moving on.

Anti-heroes are a hybrid of hero and villain. Predominantly hero because of her redeeming qualities, she also has significant flaws which are seen as negative or uncharacteristic of a hero, hence the 'anti.'

By flaw, I don't mean the kind of flaw where she fails to help an old lady cross a road one time because she was rushing to hand painkiller jelly to a kid with two broken clavicles. I mean a fundamental flaw that puts her squarely on the borderline of hero and villain.

Heroes are all full of morals and chivalry, like:

- Strength
- Courage
- Compassion
- Tactfulness

- Discipline

But anti-heroes are a different breed. While he or she might have noble intentions, his personality makes for a more niche flavor of hero that lacks the traditional 'heroism' found in your bog-standard Clark Kent. Anti-heroes are like abstract art displayed in the middle of a Renaissance exhibition.

An anti-hero does the right thing in the end like saving the heroine, but he'll have enough negative traits to balance out the good. For example, he could be:

- A chauvinist
- Arrogant
- Sexist
- Callous
- A hypocrite
- Selfish
- Self-indulgent
- Manipulative
- Weak
- Greedy
- Amoral
- Merciless

Heroic actions define a hero, making him all things good, moral and sparkly. But an anti-hero is the perfect example of a hero whose halo needs a bloody good dusting. His actions are not always good.

Anti-heroes are heroes that not only have negative personality traits but engage in bad/wrong/immoral behaviors too.

But it's not just personality traits. Anti-heroes engage in all the ~~fun behaviors too~~ bad behaviors too, like:

- Adultery
- Murder
- Theft
- Gossiping
- Excessive promiscuity
- Lying

Name your naughty behavior, and you'll find an anti-hero engaged in it.

Everybody Likes A Naughty School Boy

What is it about anti-heroes that's so appealing? I can't help myself if the protagonist is an anti-hero - I am like a salivating dog. I can't get enough of whatever it is I'm reading or watching. I'm a self-confessed anti-hero addict.

It's evolution to find your species attractive because it's how you survive. That inbuilt mechanism is wired to our genes and based on the principle of finding *ourselves* attractive. We look for a mate that embodies ourselves as well as things we don't have, things we need, and what can protect us.

Much as Superman's six-pack and silky black hair are stunningly gorgeous, would you rather have him, or Wolverine protecting you in a dark alley? I know who I'd rather have.

Superheroes in their truest form are the embodiment of perfection. They can save the girl, the city and the baby falling from the skyscraper window and still have their eyes closed and be back in time for Granny Gertie's dinner. But that's fantasy and utterly unrealistic.

Anti-heroes, on the other hand, are a much truer reflection of humanity. We, the human monkey wordsmiths of the world, are flawed. We are not perfect, and we are nothing like Superman. We mess up, make bad decisions, and sometimes, the falling baby goes kersplat because we didn't catch it in time. Oops.

Superman is a reflection of what humanity wants to be: a utopian idea and one we will likely never reach. But that's his appeal – perfection personified, an aspiration for our dodgy society.

Wolverine, on the other hand, is not perfect. He is flawed with a capital F. If you were in a dark alley, Superman's response would be to dance around like a ballerina trying to avoid the bad guy's punches for long enough that he can tie him up.

Wolverine wouldn't give a toss about the legal system or saving the hooded thug's life just to jail him. He'd knife him in the throat with his crazy metal skeleton claws and get you the hell out of there. And that flawed thinking and response is much closer to what we humans would do: attack and run.

Humanity doesn't save the bad guy and let the legal system punish the criminal because we know the legal system is faulty too. We live off hormones, and thanks to Darwin, we know the reason we incapacitate and run when the bad guy is bigger than us is because of our autonomic nervous system's fight or flight response.

Superman will always try to save a villain because to him, life is life. Wolverine doesn't care. (In Wolverine vol. 1, #1) He says, "I got no stomach for guttin' animals. People though - that's another matter."

Anti-heroes embody our darkest secrets and desires. They blur the line between what dark and twisty parts of us want, like justice without the bureaucracy of law, and what society says we should want: a trial and imprisonment.

Anti-heroes can take the bad decisions we want to make without society's judgement. The anti-hero has the affairs we can't, and stabs his boss in the eye with a fork because he's a schmuck and deserves it; he cheats, lies and steals and all to further his own wanton desires.

Anti-heroes do what we want to but never can. This is what makes them sellable, and marketable. An anti-hero has his cake, and cons his way into eating it. He is a reflection of us, and because he is flawed, we see his humanity, despite his terrible behavior.

Blur Lines Like You're Drunk

A hero has glass-clear motives. She wants to save the day, be a good person, believe in the 'cause,' and willingly sacrifice herself just to save a mewling kitten. Blah, blah, blah, yawn. An anti-hero is different. His motives are messy and complicated.

An anti-hero's motives for saving the day are not always pure.

While the catalyst for getting an anti-hero to become heroic at the climax of your story might involve love or something else positively sugar coated, their motives, (particularly early on in your stories) can be far darker.

Self-preservation, desire, revenge, and greed are all recurring motives behind an anti-hero's actions.

An anti-hero blurs the line between villain and hero, but what keeps him in the hero category is that there is a line (a moral or ethical one) he won't cross.

Character Example: Robin Hood, the Character - Robin Hood is a thief which is a villainous behavior you wouldn't typically associate with a hero. The stealing is what gives him his 'anti' side. But the reason why he steals is what gives him his 'hero' side. Robin Hood has a moral line he won't cross.

He will only steal from the rich who don't need the money so he can give it to the poor people in his village.

Blurring the line between the right motives and the wrong ones make anti-heroes fun to write. **They can do the right thing for the wrong reason, or the wrong thing for the right reason.** That complexity makes them more interesting to readers. I mean, aren't you bored of reading about a hero always doing the right thing for the right reason?

Floored By Flaws

Anti-heroes make mistakes, lots of them because they are usually motivated by personal interest rather than altruism. Put an anti-hero in a corner, and instead of sacrificing herself she'll bite like an angry Chihuahua. She's weak and concerned with self-preservation. If doing the wrong thing is easier than doing the right thing, and doing that wrong thing gets her what she wants faster, she'll do it. Over, and over, and over again. If she thinks the end justifies the means, she'll pursue it relentlessly; just like a villain.

Flawed heroes are different to anti-heroes. A flawed hero will learn from his mistakes. A flawed hero might make a mistake, but he'll only make that mistake once.

A flawed hero grows and develops during the story, his bad traits lessened, his flaws eradicated and all because at his core, he is still a hero.

Think of the flawed hero's 'flaw' as a wound - the story leads him to a place where he is healed and no longer has the wound; all that remains is a wound-free 'proper' knight-in-shining-armor hero.

The best place to find flawed heroes is in children's films and books. They're full of them because a flawed hero is more interesting than Prince Charming, but 'good' enough not to require a PG or higher rating.

Character Example: Woody a flawed hero from Toy Story, The Movie - Woody's flaw is jealousy. Woody is Andy's (the child) toy sheriff. But on Andy's birthday, a new toy (Buzz Lightyear) is given to him as a present and swiftly becomes Andy's new favorite.

Woody gets jealous, which causes him to make bad decisions and that results in both Woody and Buzz getting lost. The story revolves around the adventure the pair go on trying to return home before Andy's parents move house and they're lost forever. Woody realizes his jealous flaw, swallows his pride and works with Buzz to get them both home.

The reason he's a flawed hero and not an anti-hero is that deep down Woody is a good guy; he's jealous not out of self-interest like an anti-hero would be but because he loves Andy, which is why he

```
learns from his flaw, and stops being
jealous. An anti-hero doesn't learn.
```

An anti-hero has flaws and more. His wounds don't heal in the same way. **Instead of healing and becoming a hero, he stays wounded but makes better decisions**.

An anti-hero also has faulty logic. He will consistently make outlandish decisions while thinking they're perfectly rational. Readers know different.

There are **two kinds of faulty logic** that lead an anti-hero to **make two types of decision**:

1. Bad decisions for the right reasons
2. Good decisions for the wrong reasons

Both demonstrate an anti-hero's self-interest and generate plot fuel for us writers. Why? Because poor decision-making creates interesting situations, a shit load of conflict and an extra gourmet portion of tension. **It's also why an anti-hero has a simpler character arc because he rarely changes; he just makes better decisions.**

As a writer, you need to **orchestrate your plot so that he learns how to make better decisions.**

The above graphic illustrates the rough range of an anti-hero on the villain to hero scale.

On the anti-hero spectrum, as well as taking into account 'goodness' and 'badness,' there are two other measures to assess how good or bad your anti-hero is:

1. How bad are the methods and tactics they use to seek justice, in other words, their 'means?'

2. And the result of their actions, the 'ends?'

Using these measures, you can add a level of complexity to anti-heroes, and create a sliding scale of anti-heroism.

Let's take a couple of examples starting with the anti-heroes whose haloes only have trace particles of evil dust.

Both Batman and Robin Hood are at the top 'good' end of the anti-hero spectrum. They barely make the cut because they are almost entirely 'hero'... BUT...

Batman is on the edge of anti-heroism because while he has the qualities of a hero - saving the innocent and working to bring justice to villains - his nature is not 100% 'classic hero.' Batman is a man of the shadows and night; this in itself is a personification of his anti-heroism. It shows the reader that his methods might not always come from the pure light wielding goodness of a hero. Batman will regularly flout, break or outright ignore the law and police system to capture a villain. Tut, tut, Bat boy!

Batman's 'ends' are good: the results are heroic, but his 'means' and methods of achieving them don't always conform to 'heroism' and that makes him an anti-hero.

Similarly, **Robin Hood** is a justice seeker; he's a hero that works for the poor and the little man. But, like Batman, his means and methods are not always pure. Robin Hood has a twisted sense of justice. He believes stealing is right because he is taking money from the rich who don't need it and giving it to the poor who do.

While what he is doing is wrong (his means), his outcomes (ends) are heroic, putting him firmly at the top of the anti-hero scale with Batman.

Dexter is a character written by Jeff Lindsay, from the book *Darkly Dreaming Dexter* and the TV series, *Dexter*. He sits somewhere in the middle of the hero-villain scale. Dexter is a serial killer. He murders people in a blood-bath style way so he can satiate his murderous urges, clearly a villainous quality. He is on the extreme end of violent and is a psychopath.

But the ends or results of his bad deeds are (if you conform to his twisted sense of justice) rather good. When Miami's police fail to convict criminals, Dexter takes it upon himself to dish out a rather more permanent style of justice. He clears the streets of nasty criminals leaving Miami a better place to live.

Patrick Bateman is a character written by Bret Easton Ellis from the book and film *American Psycho*.

Bateman barely scrapes in as an anti-hero. He is right on the furthest edge of the anti-hero/villain line, mostly because he's an evil son of a bitch. Riddled with personality disorders, he is, in effect, a psychopath. However, he has one or two small redeeming qualities that just pull him into the realm of anti-hero. First, he is the protagonist of both the book and the film which makes a reader naturally empathize with his journey. There's also an implication in the film that he only imagined killing people.

Bateman is the kind of anti-hero that makes bad decisions for the right reasons. More than anything, he wants to be happy, a noble quest for sure. The problem, in part, is his personality disorder, alongside the fact he is surrounded by narcissistic elitist socialites all competing to be 'the best' and have the best things.

This need to be the best leads him into a violent, murderous killing spree. But he wants absolution from it and tries to get it by confessing his sins to friends, colleagues and random strangers. Unfortunately for Bateman, no one believes he's a killer, and so, he never gets absolution.

It's Not All Mirror, Mirror On The Wall

Your stock hero is devastatingly handsome, tall and annoyingly muscular. But with anti-heroes you don't have to be confined to standard Popeye-hero symmetry or descriptions that read like identical milk cartons. If you have an anti-hero for a protagonist, you could have an ugly, fat hero covered in spots and stinking of stale sweat.

Anti-heroes don't have to be defined by a heroic image; you can fiddle with their middles and get messy with their appearance.

Don't be restricted by any aspect of heroism, as long as your anti-hero does the right thing (in the end) you can tweak any part of their character-clay and shape it however you like.

A charming hero who happens to be ugly as sin is way more exciting than a debonair prince. Deadpool, the Marvel Universe and comic hero, is an anti-hero that saves the girl he loves, but his face and body get mutilated during the process of obtaining his super power. See? Much more interesting!

Anti-Arcs – The Character Arc That Isn't

An anti-hero, like any other hero, protagonist or villain, needs a character arc. It's character development 101. But their arc also happens to be the easiest to create. Like any character, there needs to be lots of ups and downs on their journey through the plot to make the arc-change believable. **Anti-heroes are leopards. They can't change their spots. Your anti-hero should start more 'anti' than hero, and end up as the story hero but with his 'anti' personality intact.**

If you castrate the arrogant, self-centered, negative trait out of them at the end of the book, then you're removing the one thing that makes them 'anti' and turning them into a flawed hero.

Character Example: Dexter from the TV series Dexter - Dexter is at risk of his real identity being revealed throughout all eight seasons. In the end, Dexter decides to fake his death and disappear forever to protect his family from himself and his terrible crimes.

Dexter makes the right choice to leave and protect his family, making him a hero. He sacrificed his happiness to save that of his child and girlfriend. But he doesn't change; he's still a murderer with murderous tendencies, he just made the right decision. Call it karma, or penance, but this shows **anti-heroes don't always get the perfect ending, even when they make the right choice.**

Right Thing, Wrong Thing

But Dexter's ending isn't the only way anti-heroes can do the right thing.

For example, they can:

- Save the girl but not the best friend/mother/mentor (insert any other character that's important to the protagonist)
- Defeat the villain but lose something or someone in the process
- Sacrifice someone or something to win
- Do the right thing but return to their old life and style immediately after
- Do the wrong thing but win anyway

Anti-heroes start out doing the wrong thing but, during your story, something needs to trigger a change that leads to them to make the right decision (and do the right thing). It's the journey and the experiences they have in your plot, that will trigger this change just like heroes have a tipping point where they move from reaction to action.

With any story arc, you need to plot the character change throughout the story:

- Usually at 50% of the way through a story, the anti-hero will begin to question themselves.
- 60-80% through your book your anti-hero will start making better decisions.
- And at 85-95% of the way through, they will make the redeeming decision that leads them to save the day and retain their anti-hero status.

Character Example: Deadpool the character from The Marvel Universe, Deadpool, The Movie- bad decisions for the right

reason- 1% into the film we are introduced to Deadpool the character. His job is a mercenary (a typically evil job), although early on we see he isn't all bad because he doesn't beat or kill his victims - he scares them into compliance. But this is his first bad decision - his job.

5% - he meets his true love, cue the montage of them falling in love.

8% - he is told he has incurable cancer.

10% - he makes bad decision number two - he decides to leave his girlfriend, although it's for the right reason (to save her the pain of watching him die).

20% - he is cured of cancer by the villain (Ajax) and, as a result, made into Deadpool (with massive facial and full-body skin deformities).

25% - good decision gone bad number three. He attempts to go back to his girlfriend but can't talk to her because of his new physical deformities. She doesn't know he's cured.

30% - good decision for the wrong reason - Deadpool starts pursuing Ajax to fix his deformities so he can return to his girlfriend.

30-80% - cat and mouse pursuit, chasing Ajax and failing to apprehend him.

80% - Ajax goes to Deadpool's best friend's bar and discovers Deadpool's weakness - his girlfriend.

85% - Deadpool's best friend tells him about Ajax's visit. Finally, he makes the right decision for the right reason. He goes to find his girlfriend to tell her she's in danger and protect her (this is now three years after he disappeared from her flat and she assumed he died).

90% - but when Deadpool gets to her place of work, Ajax has already kidnapped her and is demanding Deadpool come and get her so he can kill him.

95% - good decision two, Deadpool finally enlists help and saves the girl.

Deadpool doesn't make a good decision for the right reason until 85% of the way through the film.

The final trigger to get him to change his ways is the threat of danger to someone he loves.

Just like villains, anti-heroes have weaknesses, and using their weakness is the easiest way to get them to make a better decision because usually it comes from their core or values.

It's the threat of danger to the thing they want most that causes a change in an anti-hero's decision making.

STEP 7 – All About Anti-heroes Summary

- Anti-heroes are a hybrid of hero and villain. They retain hero status because, despite negative flaws, poor behavior, and bad choices, they make the right decision and do the right thing in the end. There is also a line, a moral or ethical one, that they won't cross.

- An anti-hero's motives for saving the day are not always pure.

- Flawed heroes are still heroes. Their flaws are reduced; they grow and develop during the story because, at their core, they are still heroes.

- Anti-heroes either make bad decisions for the right reasons or good decisions for the wrong reasons.

- Anti-heroes have simpler character arcs because they rarely change, they just make better decisions.

- Anti-heroes don't have to be defined by heroic descriptions; you can mess with their appearance.

- Even though an anti-hero redeems themselves, if you have to remove the 'anti' to make them a 'hero' then they aren't an anti-hero at all: they're a flawed hero.

- To understand your anti-hero better, ask yourself these questions: how bad are the methods he uses to seek justice and how good are the results he gets?

- Just like villains, anti-heroes have weaknesses. Using their weakness is the easiest way to get them to make better decisions because usually, it comes from their core values and behaviors.

- It's the threat of danger to the thing they want most that causes a change in decision making.

- Anti-heroes embody our darkest secrets and desires. They blur the line between what dark and twisty parts of us want, like justice without law and what society says we should want: a trial and imprisonment of criminals.

Questions To Think About

Find three examples of anti-heroes in your genre. Ask yourself the following:

What kind of faulty decisions do they make?

What's their flaw?

How do they redeem themselves?

STEP 8 – Moustaches And Cackles – AKA The Clichéd Villain

You know when you're in the cinema watching a proper funny comedy and some idiot in the back row is cackling at the top of their lungs, putting Cruella to shame? Well, I'm that idiot. My laugh would rival even the best villains.' But I'm allowed to laugh like that because

a) I'm happy having a clichéd laugh.
b) I'm not a villain.

At least not today; I've had my coffee allowance. Your villain, however, is most definitely *not* allowed to laugh like that. It's a cliché, and nobody likes a cliché, especially when it's a really overdone one.

The problem is, to create credible evil characters you have to wade through a minefield of unexploded clichés. Danger zone is an understatement. We have been lazy; the years of hero worship and focus on protagonists has resulted in neglected villains and an over-reliance on classic clichés. Well, screw that, and screw the hero too. Long live the Evil Queen.

Clichés VS Tropes

The thing about clichés is that they get everyone's knickers in a right twist. I hear it all the time: clichés are bad, they are Jack Frost's ice covered boogers and you can't have boogers in your book. But before you throw out all the clichés, you need to understand that the reading population only think clichés are bad because they're bored of seeing the same storylines over and over again.

BUT.

And, this is a colossal but, writers often confuse clichés with tropes and they are very different. Clichés make books plummet down the charts, but tropes will have it soar like Superman on speed because it's delivering what the market wants and expects.

Clichés are words, phrases, expressions or scenes that have been overused to the point they've become predictable and unoriginal.

Classic examples include:

- 'Objection' used in a court scene when the prosecutor is losing
- The priest saying 'Does anyone object?' and the protagonist's true love bursting into the church
- A villain or a witch with a 'muhahaha' laugh or a cackle
- They all lived happily ever after
- And then I woke up and realized it was all a dream

Did they make you cringe? Cause I felt dirty having to write them. Tropes are different.

Tropes are reoccurring themes, concepts and patterns usually found embedded within genres. Tropes help you identify what genre you're reading. What separates a trope from a cliché is that a trope can be used over and over again, as long as it's told in a novel way each time and it won't piss off your readers.

When you read the list of trope examples below, you should be able to reel off half a dozen books in the relevant genre that uses them, and I bet each story you think of is completely different.

Classic Trope Examples:

Young Adult Tropes
- Orphan protagonist or distant parents
- Love triangles
- A graduation ceremony

Fantasy
- The chosen one
- The one magical sword/potion/device that will save the world and is conveniently difficult to locate
- Prophecy

Crime
- A dead body discovered at the start of a novel
- A crime fighting detective overly dedicated to the job
- A maverick detective
- A murderer either arrested or killed at the end of the book
- Serial killers

Romance Tropes
- Boy meets girl
- Enemies to lovers
- Forbidden lovers
- Matchmaker
- Societal class divide between love interests
- Happy ever after endings

Villainous Clichés

There are a ton of villainous clichés, and I won't list them all, but below is a short list, to give you a little flavor of what villain clichés look like:

- Black cats, parrots or pets of any variety attached to a villain - think pirates with parrots or Dr. Evil's bald cat in Austin Powers
- Phrases like, "I'm going to destroy the world" or "I'm going to rule the world"
- Dark hair, dark eyes, dark outfits. Anything associated with the color black
- Slick hair
- Disfigurements or scars
- Swagger
- Excessive arrogance
- Excessively charming
- Mental health disorders
- Lairs/dungeons/penthouses
- Delusions of grandeur
- Witches with black hats, pointy noses and a wart
- Witches with cackles or villains that go 'muhahaha'
- Excessive hyperbolic monologues
- Manners or posh accents (particularly British or Eastern European)
- A classical music lover
- A love of red wine / Chianti
- Fireplaces with roaring fires and logs
- Massive self-portraits hanging in lounges, lairs or offices
- Thrones or wing backed chairs
- Henchmen (although this one can also be a trope)

- If not henchmen, then minions or some kind of second in command that does all their bidding
- Evil with no motive
- Befriends the hero
- A villain that reveals his plan before acting on it
- Smoking
- Shaved heads
- Formerly imprisoned
- Loves their mother excessively
- Runs a secret society
- Bad childhood
- Voices in their head
- Extremist viewpoints

Villain Trope Examples

General Tropes
- Henchmen (genre dependent)
- Power hungry
- Wants to win at all costs
- Killing someone innocent

Dystopian
- A dinner feast/party/ball or major celebration hosted by the villain and representing the class difference
- A villain with a hard to argue with reasoning for the dystopian societal system

Thriller
- Helicopter or speed boat, but some swanky method of escape
- Psychopath/sociopath
- Scantily clad women, serving a villain's every desire

Fantasy

- Wolves, dragons and snakes
- Dark magic

Unless you're writing children's stories, which I'll come to in a minute, avoid clichés like the plague… did you see what I did there! *Snigger*

Generally, clichés are bad. But tropes – tropes are useful because they identify your book's genre. Tropes create a gnawing in your reader's gut. A sense of familiarity they can't quite locate. A comfortable warmth of knowing they're home. You want them to have a, 'wait a bloody minute; I know what's going to happen,' moment and then hit them with a twist they never saw coming. That's what keeps a reader running back for more.

Don't get me wrong; you can use a cliché. There's nothing wrong with the occasional cigar puffing, whiskey drinking mobster sat by a roaring fireplace. But everything in moderation, folks.

Don't have all the clichés or all the tropes in one story. If your story is unique, you can get away with a sprinkling of clichés; but use them sparingly.

You don't need to use *all* the tropes in one go either, think of tropes as diamonds. Every girl wants a diamond, but no one's rich enough to buy an entire ball gown made of ten carat diamonds, and if you are, bugger off and stop ruining my analogy.

If you write children's fiction or fairy tales you need to use at least one happy ever after cliché because we can't give the little rugrats Stephen King style nightmares now, can we? With the exception of a happily ever after ending, kids don't need clichés in their stories any more than adults do. Although they are used, there are fewer and fewer clichés in the market as the rise of strong female characters like Merida from *Brave* or Anna and Elsa from *Frozen* increase in popularity.

Clichés are tired. Euthanize them. Regularly. But tropes are the bricks and mortar that build the foundations of genres. They are tried and tested plot devices that work. Go forth and sprinkle tropeorific sauce all over your manuscripts.

Treading The Fine Line Between Cliché And History

There is a silky thin line between cliché and historical accuracy and we writers need to pay attention to it. See, some clichés have come into existence through historical fact. Take gangsters and cigar smoking: iconic, but also a cliché. But it didn't start that way. Between 1920 and 1940, mob rule was rife, especially in America, England and Italy.

It's the era we think of when someone says 'gangster.' But the cigar wouldn't have been a cliché then because it was popular culture.

Cigarettes in the 1920s weren't seen as cancer-inducing death sticks like they are today. It was fashionable, trendy, a sign of power. The cliché only came into existence with the introduction of mass media, the popularity of films like *Scarface* and *The Godfather* and the resulting explosion of gangster films, TV and books.

If you're going to write a gangster novel set in the 1920s then you're going to have to pay attention to historical accuracy. Readers pick historical fiction because they want to be immersed in that era. Believe me, they are hawks and will spot any error in historical accuracy. Avoiding a cigar-wielding gangster because it's a cliché *now* will remove your authenticity and credibility as a historical fiction writer. Your novel needs to suit the era or period it's set in, irrelevant as to whether you're creating a cliché.

Not all clichés are bad. Don't be afraid to give the occasional nod to a cliché if it's derived from history. Readers will expect it, and in fact, you'll be criticized more for not using them.

Avoiding The Cliché Curse

You get the difference; you know your clichéd Christmas jumper from your standard crime worthy serial killer. But how do you avoid sprinkling your literary darlings with cliché glitter?

Some clichés are based on historical fact. In this instance, you can't always avoid a cliché because you still need to create authenticity in your work. So the occasional cliché, especially when it represents a factual piece of history, is fine.

Much as I'd love to hand you a checklist of what to avoid, the book market and particularly genres, are constantly evolving. What I write today might be obsolete in a year's time, and back in fashion again three years after that. Instead, I'll give you the tools to stay clued in yourself.

The Tools

Tool 1: Nothing is going to substitute you going out and educating yourself on the genre you write. Go. Read books. ALL THE BOOKS. I don't mean one or two either. I mean read the motherload of books from your genre so that you can identify both the tropes you need to include and the clichés you need to avoid. The more you read your genre, the more obvious it will become. Make it a game: spot as many patterns and repetitions across the books in your genre as you can.

Tool 2: Stay conscious while you read. Instead of switching off and reading for leisure, read every sentence. The more aware you are, the slower you'll read, the easier it is to spot patterns.

Tool 3: This one's important. Take notes, highlight sections and use Post-Its as bookmarks so you can come back to the pages you've marked.

Tool 4: Get to grips with your emotions. Think about your genre and any common tropes or clichés you've noticed wriggling into your market. How do these reoccurring tropes or clichés make you feel? If some make you rage worse than Hulk, while the others make you swoon with genre love, then pay attention.

Anything that makes you swoon you need to dissect, learn from and implement the techniques. These are tropes. But anything that makes you rage like Hulk you can bin: they're clichés.

Tool 5: The delightful beast that is Amazon. Check your genre (and sub genre's) top 100 books. Time is always tight as a writer, so pick five to read and analyse. Two from the top ten, two from the mid-range listings and one from near the 100th position.

Tool 6: Use the list of clichés in the previous chapter to review your villain and check whether you've included any.

Tool 7: The things you need to pay attention to while reading in your genre:

Protagonist - Is there a pattern to her personality? For example, in YA dystopian novels, like *The Hunger Games* and *Divergent*, both the protagonists are feisty, strong-willed rebels.

The Love Interest - As above - what similar traits do the characters have?

The Villain - Again, what traits do the characters have? How are they introduced? What do they want? And how are they killed or captured?

Themes - Are there reoccurring themes running through the books?

Settings - Is there anything atmospheric the authors in your genre do, or particular senses they try to engage? You also need to look at the physical setting. Take books in war zones - there's often military equipment or vehicles, or maybe they're set in deserts.

Plot, Pace And Tension - Does your genre use a particular pace or tension arc for the villain? Is it fast at the start, slow in the middle and fast at the end or something else?

Phrasing - Sometimes - although the way authors construct their sentences will vary - there can be a particular tone or phraseology you find in a genre. For example, YA books often use the phrase 'I realized' because teenage protagonists are young and inexperienced, and therefore often have emotional revelations throughout the novels.

Reader Emotion - Do you get the same sense of feeling when reading the books - is a horror author making you scared, or creeped out? Or perhaps just shocked and disgusted?

Hook And End - is there a particular hook that's used? Maybe a dead body appears in crime, or in YA a graduation ceremony.

If you've read this and are now freaking out because you have a ton of clichés in your story, fear not, dear writer. You don't have to remove every single cliché. If you've used them in moderation, they fit a historical context, or they are subtle enough your beta readers skim over them, leave them be.

STEP 8 - Moustaches and Cackles – AKA The Clichéd Villain Summary

Clichés are words, phrases, expressions or scenes that have been overused to the point they're as dull as watching paint dry. They're predictable and unoriginal.

- Tropes are reoccurring themes, concepts and patterns usually found embedded within genres. Tropes help you identify what genre you're reading. What separates a trope from a cliché is that a trope can be done over and over again, as long as it's told in a novel way each time.

- Unless you write kids' books, clichés are bad, tropes are good. Say it. Say it again, and then tattoo it on your sweaty forehead.

- And now I contradict myself because everything in moderation is fine. If you have to use a cliché, pretend you're on a Vogue runway, hide it with a fancy outfit and make it look different.

- If you write genre fiction, make sure you study your genre's tropes so you can use them wisely. Tropes are tropes for a reason, they work. People like them. Don't be an idiot and avoid them all to be unique because you'll write yourself out of your genre.

Questions To Think About

Name five tropes and five clichés from your genre.
Name three villains that are not clichéd in your genre.

STEP 9- The Idea Of Fear Is All You Need

Fear is important. It's as important to you as a writer as it is to your readers. Alongside conflict, fear drives the plot, emotion, and tension in the book. I'm not going to teach you how to write horror or scary plots, but there are principles we can take from creating fear that will help in the construction of your villain.

Fear (among other emotions) *can* be one of the drivers for the climax of your book.

If you're four, you might poop your pants over the bogeyman. After all, he's one scary mofo, all spindly, and slimy and full of decaying teeth. You've never seen him mind, but you know, with all certainty, that he exists because momma said if you put one step wrong, then he's coming for you.

At some point around eight or nine, adult logic kicks in and you realize momma played you; the bogeyman doesn't exist. In fact, he never existed. All he was, was a seed. A bogey-seed planted in your imagination that multiplied like territorial weeds on steroids. Your brain does the rest. One tiny seed and it creates a mountain of ideas, dark crevasses, demons, claws and spiders' legs.

We don't need real monsters to scare us; they're already in our heads.

Even though as adults we know there are evils, and criminals in the world, we're pretty good at shoving our heads in the sand and pretending bad things happen to other people. They don't happen to us. Right? Right?! Hmm.

Because society's beaten over the head by negativity, news stories, and terrible occurrences, all the fodder you need to grow your villains into scary literary beasts is buried deep in your reader's subconscious. Tug on a couple of threads stitched by reality and bam, the reader thinks your villain is terrifying and realistic.

Readers don't need villains to be scary; they need the idea of a villain and the idea of fear.

Psychologists will tell you that thinking or imagining an activity, like playing tennis, will light up the same areas of the brain as when you actually play tennis, albeit to a lesser extent.

What does that mean for you as a writer? It means you can forget about augmented reality, and you don't need to invent 4G cinema headsets to go with your book either, although those things would be awesome so you should probably do them anyway. But if you want to terrify your readers, **all you need is for them to 'think fear.'** If the protagonist is real to the reader and you create genuine emotions in the protagonist, then your reader's heart rate will pump at the same pace as your hero's.

What's In A Fear?

Fear is an emotion caused by a *perceived* threat of the danger of pain or harm. 'Perceived' because fears can arise even when there is no *actual* threat of harm or danger, because **most of the time, fear is irrational.** I mean, what's a coin sized spider going to do to me? If I throw a flimsy sandal at it, it's totally screwed. Yet, because of its hairbrush like legs which move at the speed of light, I squeal like a six-year-old and run away.

Fear is irrational, but that's its gift to writers. We don't need to create real fear; we just need to create the idea of

fear because a reader's irrational mind will do the rest for us.

Steal With Pride - Physiological VS Psychological

There are some moments you never forget when you're watching a film or reading a book because they give you pure clarity: an epiphany.

The Blair Witch Project came out in 1999; I was only 12, so I wasn't allowed to watch the film. But I didn't need to. My dad had watched it, and I'd seen the trailers. Everyone was raving about it, and I wanted to know what the fuss was about. I asked my dad if it was as scary as everyone was making out. He said yes. I was unconvinced having watched the trailer and seen a lot of running around, twig snapping and heavy breathing but no monsters. How could it be scary if there were no monsters? So I asked him one last question,

"But, Dad, what did you actually see?"

"Well, you don't 'see' anything."

Cue fireworks, mind explosions, and my brain shattering into a thousand pieces because that response blew my twelve-year-old storytelling mind to pieces.

After a few minutes of me stuttering out, "But, but, but…" I realized something very fundamental.

Fear doesn't exist; it's just an idea in someone's head. That's why all our fears are so different.

Horror has always worked in cycles, for example moving between blood, gore and monsters that you can see, feel and touch, which I call that physical fear – to

more unseen, supernatural type horror that I call psychological horror.

The Blair Witch Project, along with the *Sixth Sense,* were two key films that helped nudge the industry back towards psychological fear.

To create psychological fear, *The Blair Witch Project* got smart with camera angles and created a series of implications and insinuations without ever showing a thing. **This is a lesson we should take from film and put into our books: implication and insinuation are as scary as words and images.**

A reader's imagination is stronger and more powerful than our words will ever be. Work with it, use their imagination to your advantage.

Fear Has And Is Constantly Changing

Fear isn't the same anymore. It's been rewritten by changes in society and the mass media. Our inbuilt fear manual has changed. Physiological fear of the things that go bump in the night is now the equivalent of being scared of a fluffy bunny rabbit.

Writers can see the movement change too. Although the cycle started in the film industry, the concept of psychological fear has leaked into the publishing industry. For example, in the early 2010s *Gone Girl* by Gillian Flynn, *Before I Go to Sleep* by S.J. Watson and *The Girl on The Train* by Paula Hawkins were released. All top selling psychological novels.

Example: Guinea Pigs by James Howell – James Howell, author of Guinea Pigs and the Disturbed Girl trilogy, is one of my favorite authors. He uses both physiological fear and psychological fear.

"One of the hyenas clamped its mouth over her face and took out her eyeball. The other animal chewed off her nose and lips. Her leg throbbed, the femoral artery ruptured and her life squirted away in thick red jets." **James Howell, *Guinea Pigs*, p.115.**

It has gore, but that's not what creates the sphincter tightening scare factor. The context surrounding it does. The woman being eaten was alive and had been purposefully paralyzed (something that we as readers knew she was terrified of). The killer paralyzed her, so she had to watch herself get eaten.

Read that quote again knowing she's afraid of being paralyzed and is awake watching her flesh get masticated by hyenas. Doesn't that make it that bit scarier?

Four things make that section from *Guinea Pigs* psychologically scary:

1. We as readers knew she was afraid of being paralyzed.

2. There was nothing she could do to save herself; there was no hope because her death was inevitable.

3. She was vulnerable.

4. There was a gruesome gore factor added on top of all the other psychological factors.

Points 1, 2 and 3 are all emotional states, nothing to do with gore, and all to do with emotion. It's the gore that gives the scare factor its context.

> **Psychological fear is about the emotional state your characters (and therefore your readers) are in.**

Sense The Fear

We have five senses for a reason. Be clever, do the good writer thing; **use all five senses in your writing. It's important anyway, but even more so when you're trying to create fear.**

Think about it: what happened to you the last time you were afraid? It's your senses that kick in and tell you to be afraid. Fear isn't flat. It's sharp and breathless and tingly.

This is the age-old writing adage of 'show don't tell.' 'Show' doesn't mean you have to put your serial killer front and center of every chapter. Like Anton Chekhov's famous quote says, *"Don't tell me the moon is shining; show me the glint of light on broken glass."*

It's the same for villains, scary monsters and creating fear. **Don't tell me the killer is standing in front of you holding a knife covered in blood. Show me the table where the knife used to sit, and a trail of blood droplets on the floor that finishes at your feet. Let me hear the creak of floorboards or the click of a lock that no one's had a key to for a decade.**

When you're afraid your face turns white, you blink rapidly, and beads of sweat run down your back tightening your muscles. **Fear is a physical reaction heightened by your senses. Your villain needs to provoke these kinds of**

reactions in your protagonist to get your reader to feel. I recommend studying *The Emotion Thesaurus* by Angela Ackerman and Becca Puglisi for more detail.

Use the senses to heighten the protagonist's (and therefore the reader's) state of fear.

One of the arts to creating psychological fear is to make the reader know something awful or scary is coming but withhold enough information that they don't know what, why or when. Just like the music in a film reaching fever pitch and then dropping to silence. *The Blair Witch Project* is the perfect example of this. The entire film is spent knowing something awful is hunting them but not knowing what it is.

Withholding information purposefully, misdirecting, or only giving a hint at evil is enough to make a villain scary.

You can also use the environment, the setting, and pathetic fallacy to personify fear and the emotion you want your reader to feel. Just avoid clichés like conveniently timed claps of thunder.

Obstacles And Fear

Protagonists need a myriad of difficult-to-overcome obstacles and barriers during your plot. **Reaching the climax of your story should be hard for your hero,** and the source of those obstacles should be your villain or antagonist.

What's even more effective at creating tension is if:

a) The obstacles themselves are scary, for example, having to traverse the side of a grumbling volcano covered in pissed off crocodiles, razor blades and needles filled with the plague (or insert other genre-relevant scary thing).

b) Your obstacle isn't scary necessarily, but your protagonist is scared of whatever the obstacle is. For example, your villain stole the hero's girlfriend and locked her up at the top of a glass-floored tower 300 floors high and the hero happens to have a phobia of heights.

While some may be scared of heights, most aren't. But that doesn't matter. **If your protagonist is scared, then it's a barrier, and you can use his fear of it to project onto the reader.**

Even if you write romance, you *could* use **tension related fear in the climax of your book.** For example, perhaps the climax of your story is the protagonist's love interest finally confessing his love and asking for her hand in marriage. But your protagonist is afraid of commitment. Your reader wants them to get married, but for that to happen, your protagonist needs to get over her fear of commitment. In this instance, the villain responsible for her fear is an inner demon.

Just Keep Believing

Believability is crucial to creating fear. **If your reader doesn't believe what you're saying, they won't feel any fear, nor will they see your villain as scary.**

Some of the scariest stories are those that are the closest to reality, the ones that could almost be true.

It's why we have seen an increase in films that have terrorists for villains. The first time I saw a movie with terrorism based in London (a city close to my hometown), I felt uncomfortable.

That particular film was called *London Has Fallen.* Typically, cheesy action films like that don't make me bat an eyelid.

They're fun because they're not real, but this time it was British buildings and British soil, real close to my home, being blown up, not something I was used to. That made it much more real, more believable and therefore scarier.

It was less about the visual of the buildings being blown up (although that certainly helped make it oh so real to me) nor was it the people being shot that made it scary; it was the implication that

a) It's easy to blow up British soil.
b) It really can happen because look, it's happening right in front of me on screen.

That was enough to plant the idea in my head temporarily, and all you need is an idea.

Make Them Unbeatable

I've talked about the importance of making sure your villain appears unbeatable in STEP 5. But I'm highlighting it again here because having an unbeatable villain increases the fear factor.

The barriers (as well as the villain) your protagonist overcomes in the climax need to appear insurmountable. If they aren't then your reader won't believe in your protagonist's struggle to win.

Your hero needs to find it difficult enough to beat your villain that they have to undergo some character change (character arc) to beat them.

Your hero can beat your villain, but not in his current state. He must grow, change, defeat his fears and develop his arc to win.

STEP 9 –The Idea Of Fear Is All You Need
Summary

Readers don't need real monsters to scare them; monsters are already in their head.

- Readers just need the idea of a villain to be scared.

- Psychologists will tell you that thinking or imagining an activity, like say playing tennis, will light up the same areas of the brain as when you actually play tennis, albeit to a lesser extent.

- Fear is an emotion caused by a perceived threat of pain or harm; fear is irrational.

- The film industry cycles between different types of horror and fear. Psychological and physiological are the most relevant to novel writers.

- It's not what you can see that's scary but what you can't. This is psychological fear.

- We should learn from films; we can use their tactics of implication and insinuation to induce fear.

- A reader's imagination is stronger and more powerful than our words will ever be. Work with it and use their imagination to your advantage.

- Use all five senses in your writing.

- Withhold information purposefully. Misdirection and a hint at evil is enough to get readers twitchy.

- If your protagonist is scared, your reader will be too. But if your reader doesn't believe what you're saying, they won't feel a thing.

- What creates the sphincter tightening scare factor is not the gore but the context surrounding it.

- Psychological fear is about the emotional state your reader is in.

Questions To Think About

Take three heroes and villains from your favorite genre. What are the heroes afraid of? And how do the villains use that against them?

Using those three examples above, can you find examples in the books where the author has used the senses to heighten the atmosphere?

STEP 10 – A Villain's Mental Health

Let me start by saying you'll hear a change of voice in this chapter. Having studied psychology for over six years, I take mental health, the debilitating effects it has as well as the well-being of sufferers, seriously. I've avoided joking or silly analogies entirely in this chapter. **Think of this chapter as a reference section for when you need it.**

Whether or not mental health disorders should or shouldn't be used to create sinister villains isn't up for debate. They *are* used, whether anyone likes it or not, and frequently used too. Let me be clear; I am **not** suggesting people or characters with mental health issues are all villains or antagonists. What I am saying is that **some** of the great villains in literary and film history have these disorders. **What's unfortunate is that most of the time they're used in a clichéd or subtly discriminatory way.**

I've tried for the majority of this book not to impose 'my' opinion, or at least not impose it as the right and only opinion, as there are a hundred ways to skin a villain, and this book is showing you just some of them. But on this occasion, I am going to stand on my overly shiny soap box and say my piece.

There's nothing wrong with using mental health disorders as a characteristic trait of any character. BUT, too often, they are based on stereotypes and myth. Which, when a film or book goes viral in the mass media, only leads to more prejudice, ignorance, and confirmation of incorrect stereotypes. That's why I've included this chapter, which has been consulted on by a clinical psychologist so that we writers can sharpen our pen-pickets and take a stance against ill-informed character creation.

If you're going to create a villain with a mental health issue, make sure you know what you're talking about before you accidentally stigmatize a sector of society.

Why Stereotype?

Stereotypes are used because they dumb down complex concepts. They're sweeping generalizations made to simplify behavior or traits we can't get our heads around. Have you ever wondered if we're closer to being computers than humans? Think about it. We can be hypnotized, brainwashed and reprogrammed to conform to peer pressure. We don't make our own minds up anymore, society does. We're programmed to think anorexic waif forms and materialism should be celebrated.

In fact, we're so tightly wrapped up in expectation and normalcy, we think anything that has even a modicum of difference is scary, weird, evil or unacceptable. **Which is why we are sheep-robots; we only accept people that fall within a tightly controlled set of deviations. Sufferers of mental health disorders often produce behaviors that deviate from acceptable norms, and that's why they're so often used for villains because villains deviate from the norm too.**

Classic - Like Trends, Friends And Mozart

Sadly, there are a lot of mental health disorders, far too many to examine in one book on creating villains. There's a huge variety of disorders used across film and TV, but most commonly, it's personality disorders which are used as the basis of villain creation.

If you want an authentic and believable villain, who has a mental health disorder, you need to portray the mental health disorder in an authentic way. That could mean anything from medication, the range of symptoms they experience, triggers and patterns of behavior and how they relate to people.

For more character related analysis related to traits and disorders check out *The Writer's Guide to Character Traits* by Dr. Linda N. Edelstein. It's a great blend of psychology infused with the writer's perspective.

The Writer's Guide To Psychology by Carolyn Kaufman is also a fantastic resource to ensure authenticity to both your characters and any treatments or scenes around their illness; you can find it here.

Schizophrenia

The representation of schizophrenia in film and media feels like nails down a chalkboard for me because it's often confused with multiple personality disorder (MPD, often known as split personality disorder). The two disorders are very different.

Schizophrenia is not the same thing as multiple personality disorder.

Another misperception of schizophrenia is that sufferers are violent. They are not. Some symptoms can lead to aggressive or violent behavior, but this is rare.

Schizophrenia is a disorder of the mind often characterized by positive or negative symptoms which affect how you think, feel or behave.

Most people think schizophrenia is rare. But it's not rare at all. The prevalence of schizophrenia (and by prevalence, I mean anything from one or two symptoms up to full diagnosis) is around 1 in 100 adults.

The Positive Symptoms:

Not everyone suffers from all the symptoms.

- Delusions
- Hallucinations
- Disorganised speech or behavior

Hallucinations can affect any of the senses including auditory, visual, tactile, gustatory and olfactory.

Audible and visual hallucinations are the most commonly occurring hallucinations, and they can take any form. This includes voices you both recognize and ones you do not. Tone, pitch, content and even language vary from person to person i.e. command hallucinations where a voice will command the individual to commit an act, or give a running commentary. Auditory voices can also be in the first or third person i.e. talking about the individual.

Delusions are the beliefs that a schizophrenic person has. These beliefs don't match the way other people see the world. For example, they could be paranoid and believe that people, aliens, the government, friends or even family are plotting against them. They could also have delusions of grandeur where a sufferer believes they are famous.

Disorganized speech and behavior varies from person to person. Some people might slow down their speech; others might speed up. Sentences might make perfect sense one minute and then be jumbled and incoherent the next.

The Negative Symptoms:

- Slow labored movements
- Variation to normal sleeping pattern
- A drop or total lack of motivation
- Poor hygiene
- Lack of speech

- Difficulty goal setting or organizing
- Lack of eye contact
- A change to normal body language
- Reduced range of emotions (emotional apathy)
- Less interest in socializing or hobbies
- Low sex drive

These negative symptoms (although they seem less severe) are often perceived as more significant by patients because they last for longer periods than the positive symptoms.

Schizophrenia has a high rate of comorbidity which means that people with schizophrenia usually have other disorders too. Most often these are: *substance abuse, anxiety, and depression. But other comorbidities like OCD (obsessive compulsive disorder), PTSD (post-traumatic stress disorder), and panic disorder are found in patients with schizophrenia.*

What Writers Need To Know

- If you create a villain with schizophrenia, remember that sufferers are rarely violent. If you intend for your villain to be violent, find another reason for the violence.

- Not every schizophrenic has every symptom, and the symptoms, particularly the hallucinations and delusions, are not continually present.

- People with schizophrenia often suffer from more than one mental health disorder, so consider whether you need to include another disorder when creating your villain. Similarly, people can also experience unpleasant side effects from medication.

- Sufferers use a range of other coping strategies to manage the symptoms i.e. listening to music via headphones or sleeping to drown out the voices.

- Schizophrenia can also be triggered by traumatic experiences i.e. child abuse.

Where to find representations of schizophrenia in literature and film:

The Green Goblin from *Spider-Man* has schizophrenia. Films that include an exploration of schizophrenia but not necessarily through villains include *A Beautiful Mind*, *Donnie Darko*, *K-Pax*, *A Scanner Darkly*, and *Shutter Island*.

Last, *The Soloist* was a film based on the book of the same name by Steve Lopez, which was about the real life of Nathaniel Ayers.

Multiple Personality Disorder (MPD), Dissociative Identity Disorder (DID)

If you have a villain with MPD (also known as dissociative identity disorder (DID) or in common language, split personality), more often than not, sufferers are unable to recall their memories from their different personalities. What they 'do' and experience while in one personality will be remembered only by that personality. Once another identity takes over, the memories are forgotten.

Other symptoms can include:

- Depression
- Mood swings
- Suicidal tendencies
- Sleep disorders

- Substance abuse
- Eating disorders
- Psychotic hallucinations
- Headaches
- Amnesia
- Time loss
- Self-persecution

What Writers Need To Know

- If you have a villain with MPD, don't forget sufferers are unable to recall memories from one personality to another. What they do and experience while controlled by one personality will be remembered only by that personality. Once another identity takes over, the memories are forgotten.

- Each identity will have very distinct features, including separate genders, races, ages, sexes, gestures, mannerisms, and styles of speech. If your villain has MPD, you almost need to create an entire separate villain for each version of their personality.

Where to find representations of MPD in literature and film:

There are stacks of villains that fall into the category of multiple personality disorder. Some are depicted more accurately with regards to the disorder than others while some use it as inspiration for the character. Check out: Harvey Dent (Two-Face) from *The Dark Knight*, Dr. Jekyll from the film and originally the book *The Strange Case of Dr. Jekyll and Mr. Hyde*, Tyler Durden from *Fight Club*, and more recently Kevin from *Split*.

There are also a number heroes on the fringe (although not clinically classified) of MPD, for example, Batman and Superman.

Borderline Personality Disorder (BPD)

Borderline personality disorder (BPD) can be characterized by unstable moods, behavior, and relationships. Sufferers tend to have strong emotions and find it difficult to cope with them; there is usually a history of poor relationships, and they are highly impulsive with their behaviors.

Similar to schizophrenia, the prevalence of BPD is roughly 1 in 100. Sufferers tend to have other comorbid illnesses, which can range from *depression, substance abuse and bipolar disorder, to eating and anxiety disorders.*

Individuals with BPD have often had traumatic childhood experiences and insecure attachments with their primary caregiver. As a result, they develop an internal working model that tells them what to expect from people in relationships i.e. others can't be trusted, and they need to look after themselves. Because they haven't had appropriate emotions modeled for them in childhood, they have difficulty regulating their own emotions throughout life.

There are various symptoms:

- Intense feelings of isolation, emptiness, and boredom.
- Lacking or finding it difficult to feel empathy for anyone else.
- Negative beliefs about the self and others, which often distorts the way they feel about themselves.
- A long history of poor or unstable relationships that often swing between intense love and severe hatred.

- Changing and unpredictable moods that last from a few hours to several days.
- An intense fear of being abandoned or rejected, and extreme emotional reactions even when they perceive that might happen.
- Suffering from anxiety, worry, and depression.
- Impulsive behavior that is often risky, or dangerous and usually self-destructive. For example, drinking, drugs, unsafe sex, reckless driving and self-harm e.g. cutting.
- Often feeling hostile.
- Struggling to make life goals or plans.

What Writers Need To Know

- If you want your villain to have BPD, then consider the fact that more women than men are affected. That's not to say you can't have a male villain with BPD, but it's more common to find female sufferers.

- When thinking about your villain's personality and other traits or habits they may have, it's important to know that people with BPD often self-harm, have problems with substance abuse, and struggle to sustain relationships.

- Despite not being able to sustain relationships because of their intense emotional reactions, sufferers of BPD often crave the closeness of people. As a result, they can spend much of their lives feeling isolated.

- Sufferers tend to experience one or more of the symptoms at regular intervals, and many of them consistently throughout their adult lives.

- The causes of BPD are often (although not always) traced back to traumatic events in childhood. If your

villain has BPD, you may want to include a key event or
series of events in your character's backstory.

- Most people who have BPD suffer from regular suicidal
thoughts which coincide with their tendency to self-
harm which is a very common coping strategy.

**Where to find representations of BPD in literature and
film:**

Alex Forrest from *Fatal Attraction*, Susanna (anti-hero) from
Girl Interrupted, which is also a book written by Susanna Kaysen,
and Nurse Ratched from *One Flew Over the Cuckoo's Nest*.

Adolf Hilter and Eileen Wuornos are both real life criminals
that had BPD.

Obsessive Compulsive Disorder (OCD) And Obsessive-Compulsive Personality Disorder (OCPD)

OCD

OCD is well known for its ritualistic behaviors, which writers
and screenwriters often portray in the clichéd form of hand
washing. But there are two disorders, OCD and OCPD, that
despite being quite distinct, are often confused in film and
literature.

**OCD is an anxiety disorder, whereas OCPD is a
personality disorder.**

Obsessive-compulsive disorder (OCD) is an **anxiety
disorder** which can be identified by two things:

- The first characteristic is the obsessive, frequent and uncontrollable thoughts called obsessions that are usually unpleasant, sometimes in the form of images, and can cause feelings of anxiety and distress.

- The second characteristic is the compulsive, repetitive behaviors or mental exercises undertaken to try and relieve the unpleasant thoughts.

The two work together. For example, someone has a fear of flooding their house. This would lead them to repeatedly check their taps to ensure they were all tightly turned off. Similarly, if someone was afraid of getting sick, it could lead to ritualized cleaning.

The fears driving the obsessions are usually things like:

- Losing control
- Unwanted sexual thoughts
- Religious obsessions
- Superstitions
- Fear of being responsible for harming others
- Perfectionism
- Contamination

Compulsive behaviors are usually:

- Excessive checking or cleaning or washing
- Repeating activities numerous times or a particular number of times, like checking something three times
- Mentally going over past events or future possibilities
- Hoarding

OCPD

OCPD is different to OCD because it is a **personality disorder.** People with OCPD are concerned with controlling their environment, which is driven by a set of self-imposed and unreasonably high personal standards. They have irrational fears that others will see them as incompetent, imperfect or unsuccessful. This leads them to do things according to a set of strict rules and to suffer from intense anxiety when the rules are not adhered to.

Typically, sufferers are preoccupied with orderliness, perfectionism, and mental and interpersonal control, usually at the expense of flexibility, openness, and efficiency.

Key symptoms include:

- Often getting preoccupied with details, rules, lists, order, organization, or schedules. Usually to the extent that the major point of the activity is lost.
- Feeling that they must adhere to a stringent method for completing activities, and when they can't control those situations, becoming angry or attributing blame.
- High levels of perfectionism and standards that they hold themselves to. The standards and perfectionism are significant enough they interfere with task completion.
- Excessively devoted to work and productivity to the exclusion of leisure activities and friendships, and to the point they are usually seen as overachievers or workaholics.
- Over-conscientious, scrupulous, and inflexible about matters of morality, ethics, or values, which often leads to disregarding

others' views and results in problems maintaining relationships.

- Hoarding behavior, particularly for items that are worthless, worn out or have no sentimental value.
- A strong reluctance to delegate tasks to anyone and similarly a reluctance to work with others unless they submit to their way of doing things.
- Being miserly over money.
- Rigidness, stubbornness and inflexibility.

What Writers Need To Know

- If you have OCD, it is likely that you recognize your obsessions and compulsions are irrational but are still unable to resist them. On the other hand, those with OCPD are often not aware of how unreasonably high they've set their standards. They believe those standards are the only way to complete tasks properly.

- Consider when creating your villain that sufferers are often reluctant to seek help; perhaps your villain's disorder is a secret.

- OCPD is fairly common: up to 10% of the population have OCPD, many without even knowing it.

Where to find representations of OCD and OCPD in literature and film:

Raymond Babbitt from *Rain Man*, although he also has autism, Joan Crawford from *Mommie Dearest*, Melvin Udall from *As Good As It Gets* and Howard Hughes from *The Aviator*.

Examples of characters with OCPD are Niles Crane from *Fraser* and Monica from *Friends*. There are elements of both OCD and OCPD in Adrian Monk from *Monk*.

Narcissistic Personality Disorder (NPD)

Narcissistic personality disorder sufferers tend to have an overly inflated sense of self-importance and a deep-seated need to be admired by others. They are often devoid of empathy for anyone else. Behind all the outward facing egocentrism is an often-fragile personality with extremely low self-esteem that can be damaged further by even minor criticisms.

As a result of their inflated sense of self-importance, they often behave in ways that are deemed socially unacceptable, which causes problems for them in day to day life at work or with relationships.

Symptoms can include:

- An extreme sense of self-importance, even when it's undeserved.
- Continual exaggeration, especially when it comes to skills or talents.
- An expectation of seniority or being seen as superior when it's unwarranted.
- A preoccupation with fantasies of success and grandeur.
- A deep-seated belief of superiority and that one can only be understood by those as superior as them.
- A need to be admired.
- An entitled attitude.
- Manipulation and taking advantage of others to get what they want.

- Expectation of special treatment and favors.
- Extreme arrogance.
- Lack of empathy or understanding of anyone's needs other than their own.
- Suffering envy and believing others envy them.

What Writers Need To Know

- Deep down, their self-esteem is poor.

- Interestingly, superheroes are also frequently portrayed with NPD. Arguably, Thor has aspects of NPD, as does Hercules.

Where to find representations of NPD in literature and film:

Meryl Streep in *The Devil Wears Prada*, Gaston from *Beauty and the Beast*, Gilderoy Lockhart from *Harry Potter*, and Patrick Bateman in *American Psycho*.

Sociopathy, Psychopathy And Antisocial Personality Disorder

Trained psychiatrists and psychologists use the terms sociopathy and psychopathy interchangeably. But for this book, we will view them differently although both come under the banner of antisocial personality disorder.

There are some similarities between the two disorders, such as a disregard for the law or rules, in general, emotional apathy, violent behavior, and a corresponding lack of remorse over actions.

The differences between sociopathy and psychopathy can be seen through their demeanor.

For example, **sociopaths** are more changeable, easily agitated, and can be nervous. They are more likely than psychopaths to have bursts of uncontrolled emotions, be uneducated and live isolated from society. They are more likely to commit crimes that are disorganized and spontaneous.

Psychopaths are more controlled, and have complete emotional apathy resulting in an inability to empathize or form any relationship. They are more able to hold down a steady lifestyle because they can be highly educated, charming, and manipulative enough they can gain people's trust.

Psychopaths can meticulously plan and execute crimes meaning they are significantly harder to convict and often get away with crimes.

What Writers Need To Know

- Psychopathy and sociopathy are the two disorders used most frequently to create a villain. Be wary when using them that you don't veer into the cliché zone; make sure they still have motives for their actions.

- It's more likely that a male will be a sufferer than a female.

- Both sociopaths and psychopaths will find it difficult to hold down any form of personal relationship, but at a push sociopaths are more likely to form attachments.

Other examples of film and literature include Dexter from *Dexter*, the Joker from *The Dark Knight*, Patrick Bateman from *American Psycho*, Hannibal Lecter from *The Silence of The Lambs*, Annie Wilkes from *Misery*, Tom Ripley from *The Talented Mr. Ripley*, Charles Bronson from the film *Bronson* and some argue that Dr. Gregory House from *House* is a sociopath. Although I remain undecided on that.

STEP 10 – A Villain's Mental Health Summary

- This summary is short because there are far too many important aspects of each disorder to summarize.

- Just remember, if you choose to use a mental health disorder in one of your characters, make sure you do your research, so you don't stigmatize a sector of society.

- Top things to research include:

  - The illness in its entirety
  - Medication
  - Symptomology
  - Patterns of behavior
  - Triggers
  - Severity
  - Coping strategies
  - Reactions
  - Prevalence
  - Whether or not a person is aware of their disorder and treatments

Questions To Think About

Thinking about your favorite villains, do any of them have mental health disorders and if so, are they depicted accurately?

Ask yourself why you're choosing a mental health disorder as a characteristic. Is it to deepen the character or are you unconsciously creating a cliché?

STEP 11 - Conflict and Climax

Conflict is the foundation of every novel. Without it, your book flat lines like the Grim Reaper. No self-respecting book doctor will attempt to resuscitate it. Even a shot of conflict-adrenaline might not save it because conflict is story-oxygen, and without bags of it, your book will stay six-feet under.

If you're like me, and you love your precious little bundle of baby hero joy more than life itself, torturing them with a villain/antagonist/insert another form of conflict- shaped nappy rash can be harder than one expects.

The Source Of Conflict

While there will be many a thing in your story that causes your protagonist angst, like missing the postman, being patronized or inconveniently timed bouts of diarrhea, **the biggest source of conflict should always be your antagonist or villain.**

By that, I mean any pain your protagonist endures trying to reach his goal can't be a coincidence or the consequence of a random character's tactical wrong doings. The knife hanging out of Aunt Dotty's femoral artery needs to have been put there by the claw-hand of your villain. If your villain's a coward, then he might not push the knife in her thigh, but Aunty D's death has to be orchestrated by them.

While Kryptonite (the rock) is an issue for Superman, it's always Lex Luthor sourcing it and using it to ruin Superman's spandex.

Specificity Rules

When it comes to conflict, you can't be broad. Half measures won't work. That's like going into a bar on a Friday night and ordering half a shot of tequila. No one does that unless they're cheap, or a chicken. You're just short-changing yourself a Saturday morning hangover, and while no one wants an ethanol-induced hangover, everyone **does** want a book hangover.

The conflict has to be specific so that the hero and villain both invest in fighting each other. No one's going to get out of bed to save the world if a wild-eyed science genius 'might' release the plague, but you're not sure because your friend's sister-in-law's cousin said it might only effect ostriches. Huh? Yeah, exactly. **Be specific and link the conflict to your hero/villain's goals.**

Example: The Dark Knight, The Movie - In *The Dark Knight*, Two-Face hates Batman because he came to save him rather than saving Rachel, Two-Face's lover. Rachel dies. Two-Face blames Batman, and then the Joker convinces Two-Face to seek revenge on all the people who are vaguely at fault for her death.

This conflict is specific - Two-Face's goal is to seek revenge for everyone that failed to save Rachel and more than anyone that means Batman.

Target Like A Bullet

To motivate your hero into knuckle dusting your villain, your conflict needs to be targeted. I know that sounds 'specific,' but bite your tongue and get back in your box, because it's not the same.

It's no good your villain threatening to kill a minor character's pet snake because it would be real sad and all, but who cares.

Now, if your villain threatened to kill your protagonist's pet snake, things might be different. Especially if that snake happened to save his life as a teenager by role playing an Amazon tree rope so he could swing from a burning building with his baby brother and toy maraca in hand. Threaten to kill that snake, the one snake that means the world to him, then you got his attention.

It's the same for the villain. He has to have a realistic and targeted reason to want to kill your hero's snake – say snake's blood has the only cure to the ostrich killing plague he wants to release. Or perhaps the snake bit and killed the villain's brother before the hero owned him.

Balls To Romeo, Break Juliet's Heart

Here's where you get to wave your big authorly conductor's baton around.

Whatever you create as conflict, it needs to *mean* something. It has to be intricately linked to your protagonist and antagonist's values. What means the most to them? What's their worst fear and what or who would they die for? That's what they should be battling over.

Take me: my family and friends are everything. But I wouldn't touch my laptop or coffee either, cause then I'd have to hurt you...

Example: The Hunger Games, The Movie

In *The Hunger Games*, Katniss (the protagonist) values family above all else. So, when President Snow calls for the Reaping and her sister, Primrose, is chosen to enter a life or death competition, the conflict becomes personal. By selecting Primrose, President Snow threatens Katniss's family, making them instant enemies.

If your characters are emotionally invested in the battle, then your readers will be too.

With Realism Comes Believability

No matter how fantastical your imagination has got, you need your conflict to be realistic. Sure, a writer can make anything sound plausible, but if your hero is Superman, and you're placing a two-year-old baby against him, you're not going to orchestrate the kind of conflict you need to drive your plot on. **You need a villain who is comparable to your hero that's capable of giving him a run for his money** like Lex Luthor or General Zod.

Realism is the sum of all the other steps in creating conflict. **To create realism, make sure your conflict is specific, targeted and related to both your hero and villain's values and morals.**

And just what is a realistic ending? There's a quote from Theodore Roosevelt that I love:

"Nothing in the world is worth having or worth doing unless it means effort, pain, difficulty... I have never in my life envied a human being who led an easy life. I have envied a great many people who led difficult lives and led them well." *Reel 421,*

Theodore Roosevelt Papers, Manuscript Division, Library of Congress, Washington D.C.

Ol' Roosy might have been a politician, but this little quote is storytelling gold dust. Your heroes need to suffer for their win. Readers don't give a damn whether your hero runs off with the maiden, or if he dies pulling seaweed off his pet goldfish unless, that is, you made them invest in the hero's journey.

How did your hero get to the end? What hardships and challenges did she overcome to reach the finish line? What conflict did your villain shove in her way? Whether it's internal wallowing in daddy issues or some nuke-happy president who's willing to end it all, it doesn't matter. What's important is that the journey to the goal is a treacherous one.

Time Is Always Of The Essence

Adding time pressure into any novel builds tension and pace. Tell a guy you're going to kill his momma/sister/lover unless he does some obscure thing by 12pm, and he's going to be motivated.

Time pressure makes conflict more intense. It raises the stakes and takes away a bit more of your hero's hope.

But use it wisely, because if you use it too often, it loses its impact. Add pressure at key points for optimal effect. For example, when your hero loses a battle or someone's been kidnapped, or he thought he secured some tool which was vital to defeating the villain only now it's gone missing, how do you add time pressure? Make the bomb your villain strapped to your hero's girl start ticking. Think Keanu Reeves in the movie, *Speed.*

The point of adding a time constraint is to add pressure and build conflict. So, add it in right when your hero thinks all is lost.

If This Was Poker, I'd Be All In – Raise The Stakes Baby

Time pressure is good, but it shouldn't be the only stake you raise. Raise all the stakes. No one cares if you steal $20. Steal $200,000,000 and someone might notice. Threaten to blow up a building? Meh. Threaten to blast an entire city to smithereens then someone might care. If they don't, then blow up a country.

Raise the stakes by:

- Making whatever it is the villain is going after important to the hero.

- Adding some pressure when things get difficult.

Example: The Hunger Games, The Movie - In *The Hunger Games*, if it hadn't been Katniss's sister who was called to the Reaping, she wouldn't have sacrificed herself. Likewise, if it had been anyone other than Peeta at the end of *The Hunger Games*, she wouldn't have made the suicide pact with him; she'd have just killed him.

As the stories progress through the series, the stakes are raised because President Snow threatens more and more lives until he is willing to sacrifice any and every Panem resident to gain control and power over the city and the districts.

It's Torture Time

Torture your protagonist. Not the real fork in the eye kind of torture but the emotional, heart wrenching, life changing kind of torture. Conflict is a gift from story-hell for your protagonist; if they want to win, they should have to suffer and lose/give up/sacrifice something to beat your villain or antagonist.

This links to STEP 4 and the soul scars I mentioned. The wound your hero picks up trying to win should be in soul scar territory. It needs to change them.

It's no good stealing a used napkin off your hero and expecting him to change in a significant way to beat your villain to get it back. **Your villain needs to take everything from the hero: everything he loves, wants or will want.** Let your villain screw up the thing your hero loves most and then have your villain burn it to the ground.

Make your hero feel like there is no possibility of winning, and then when your hero is so crushed and defeated, his true hero-self will come alive, and that's when he changes enough he can defeat your villain.

Example: The Matrix, The Movie -
Agent Smith tortures Neo constantly throughout the Matrix. He kills Neo's friends, beats the snot out of him, and then kidnaps the man who saved him from the Matrix - Morpheus.

Then because Neo hasn't changed yet, Agent Smith kills him.

But because of love, and Neo's magical 'The One' powers, he comes back to life, reborn, changed, and fully enabled as The One.

But changing and moving through a hero's arc can't be easy. It has to leave a hero with a wound, whether that's physical, emotional or otherwise. Neo's wound is two-fold: growing up in the Matrix and dying before realizing he was 'The One.'

Climax That Showdown

Climax Like A Multiple O

Conflict and the climax of your book are inextricably linked. One leads to another and without both linked in a hot tub of bookalicious joy, your story won't work. **They are so intertwined, many of the same principles of conflict are translatable into your story's climax, and that's because your book is about conflict, which means your climax is too.**

Everything in your story leads to one defining moment, a crescendo of sorts. Think of it as your book's multiple O. A BIG fat juicy bookgasm. It's the defining moment your readers will never forget. Balls it up, and you lose them forever. Get it right, and you have a fan for the entirety of their short mortal lives.

What does your book's climax need to do? **One win, one loss and two characters changed forever.**

While heroes usually win, good writers wound them in the process. Why? Because that's damn good storytelling. No one would watch soap operas unless there were dramatic climaxes in each episode. Think about the end of an episode where nothing happens. You feel flat and can't be bothered to watch the next show.

And that's the point: climaxes need to grip the reader enough they would rather cut out their kidney and cannibalize it for breakfast than not finish your book.

One On One

Even if your grand finale involves a mega war between a million minions from the Underworld and an entire army of angels, the showdown still comes down to one thing:

The hero and the villain. Because that's what stories are: the interaction, relationship, impact and effect one person has on another.

Throughout your story, the conflict breadcrumbs you dropped will have produced enough drama to create the climax. During the climax, everything but the hero and villain is irrelevant. It's just stage scenery, decoration, pretty lights, tinsel and book fluff. Much needed fluff but book fluff nonetheless. So, even if your hero's mother gets a poison dart to the eye, no one cares.

Example: The Matrix, The Movie -
In *The Matrix*, all the subplots converge during the climax - the love story between Trinity and Neo, Morpheus's

escape and Cypher's betrayal. But none of that matters because we all want to know whether Neo realizes he's The One and can take down Agent Smith.

While you close off subplots in your climax, the reader focuses on your hero and villain – what they do, and what happens to them, so make sure that's what your climax focuses on.

The Hero Has To Give The Final Blow

Because your story is about your hero and villain, **whatever action is taken to annihilate the villain has to come from the hand of the hero. Likewise, the steps leading to the climax of your story need to be created by your villain.**

Example: The Matrix, The Movie - Only Neo could defeat Agent Smith, not Morpheus or the Oracle or Trinity. While those characters played a role in both bringing Neo to Agent Smith, and helping him realize who he was, it was only ever Neo that could explode Agent Smith's Matrix code.

Mess Him Up Big Style!

We know the hero is going to win (most of the time). But we've already said we don't want him to have it easy. **For your hero to win, he has to undergo a change.**

Part of his character arc must lead him to change as a person, to see the world differently, or to realize his mistakes right at the last minute; these realizations enable him to be the person he needs to be to beat your villain.

Wounding the hero could involve:

- Losing someone they love
- Having to make a choice between two people they love
- A physical injury
- A mental health injury
- Winning but at the expense of something else
- Not being able to save everyone
- Having to make a difficult decision or choice
- Losing somebody and it being their fault
- Having the person they love kidnapped or put in jeopardy because of them

Raise, Raise, Raise Like a Pole Vaulting Robber

We talked about raising the stakes to help develop conflict. But the climax is a crescendo for a reason. You have to build up to it, layering conflict, upon tension, upon pressure. **Think of your showdown as a trifle with various coatings of sweet sugary goodness. Each layer adds something a little more special until you get to taste the climatic cherry on top.**

Example: The Matrix, The Movie - Neo escapes the Matrix, then Agent Smith sends the sentinels after Morpheus's ship, but they survive. Neo gets strong and learns to fight, kill and how to enter the Matrix. Agent Smith kills Neo's friends, and so on until the big showdown in the flat corridor with Neo reading the Matrix code and handing Agent Smith's ass to him.

The Hopeless Hero Is King

Want the book stakes to be as high as they possibly can? Then make the hero feel like all hope is lost during the showdown.

Example: The Matrix, The Movie - How does Neo lose all hope? The Oracle tells him, he isn't 'The One.' She tells him not because it's true, (because it isn't) but because that's what he needs to hear at the time. Those fateful words send him on his journey to prove her wrong. It's only when Trinity declares her love for Neo, and he realizes he had to *want* and *believe* he was The One before he could come back to life and kick Smith's butt.

Add it all up, and what have you got?

Example: The Harry Potter Series - At the end of the Harry Potter books, Harry has been on a journey to gather the Horcruxes which are pieces of Lord Voldemort's soul. By destroying the Horcruxes, Harry can kill Lord Voldemort.

Raise The Stakes And Kill The Hope
The stakes get raised when Harry's closest allies die. Both Dumbledore and Professor Snape are killed just before the climax of the series, leaving Harry with little support to defeat Lord Voldemort. Harry fears all hope is lost because the final Horcrux is missing.

By The Hand Of The Hero

It's not until Harry realizes **he is** the last Horcrux, that he understands how he can defeat Lord Voldemort. And this is why J. K. Rowling's ending is so good because the only person that can kill Lord Voldemort is Harry himself. All hope is lost *and* found simultaneously. Harry has to die, but in dying, he will save everyone else.

Even though there's a battle going on in Hogwarts and lots of the secondary characters are involved, the most important part of the battle is the showdown between Harry and Lord Voldemort.

Harry has to sacrifice himself to destroy the remaining part of Lord Voldemort's soul. When he does, there is no question: Lord Voldemort's death is at the hand of Harry.

A Word On Words - The Monologue

Villains like their own hyperbole and a jolly good speech. But letting them take center stage and waffle on without any purpose will remind your readers of the time Granddad Joe came for dinner and talked extensively about his 6th year at school when he had to take the 807 bus. But in his 7th year, everything changed because the driver died and as a memorial to him they changed the route and the kids all took the 808 bus. Anyone else asleep? That's my point.

A villain's speech needs to do two things to pack the power of a literary atom bomb.

Thing One - State The Intention

The villain sits on the other side of the fence to your hero. This is the moment the bad guy makes it clear he disagrees. **Whatever his warped view of the world is, it needs conveying**. Does he think mass genocide is a weekend hobby? Tell the reader. Does he think all fluffy bunnies need shaving and their fur making into scarves for his demonic minions? The reader wants to know.

But be clear because clarity is everything. If you're writing a dystopian world, there is always a distorted version of society, often a complex one. But that doesn't mean you can't explain it simply.

Ernest Rutherford once said, "An alleged scientific discovery has no merit unless it can be explained to a barmaid." *As quoted in Einstein: The Man and His Achievement (1973) by G.J. Whitrow, p.42.*

That man was a genius. Listen to what he said.

Thing Two - Convince The Reader The Villain's Right

You need to convince the reader the villain's right, even if it's just for a second. If you can make a reader think the villain's utterly illogical, evil opinion is a good point, then you hit the jackpot. Your villain is perfected.

But how?

Using the good stuff. The pure, rational, logic that I love so much. Sure, you need to write a compelling case, but logic's beauty lies in its simplicity.

The first time I ever agreed with a villain, my whole world was rocked. I still think about that speech to this day, and it's why I've used it as an example in this section. It starts,

"Billions of people just living out their lives, oblivious."
Agent Smith, *The Matrix*.

He continues to explain that humans are a virus on the Earth and he uses an extraordinary scientific and logical argument as to why he's right, and frankly, although I maintain the fact I'm a meliorist, I still find it hard to disagree. Take a look; this video is only four minutes long: http://bit.ly/2jDAgHS

STEP 11 - Conflict And Climax Summary

- Be specific. Link the conflict to your hero/villain's goals.

- If your characters are emotionally invested in the battle, then your readers will be too.

- To create realism, make sure your conflict is specific, targeted and related to both your hero and your villain's values and morals.

- Time pressure makes conflict more intense. It raises the stakes and takes away a bit more of your hero's hope.

- You raise the stakes by making whatever it is the villain is going after important to the hero and then adding a boatload of pressure.

Climax Summary

- Your climax, no matter the theatrics and dramatic surroundings, is only ever about two people: hero and villain. Because that's what stories are: the interaction, relationship, impact and effect one person has on another.

- No matter who's fighting in the showdown, the only action that matters is what happens between your hero and your villain. Make sure the focus is on them, what they do, and what happens to them.

- Whatever action needs to happen to annihilate the villain, it has to come from the hero, and the conflict leading up to the climax has to be driven by the villain.

- For your hero to win, he has to change. Part of his character arc must lead him to change as a person, see the world differently, or realize his mistakes. These revelations enable him to be the person he needs to be to beat your villain.

- A villain's speech needs to do two things to pack the power of a literary Oscar: state the intention and convince the reader the villain is right.

Questions To Think About

What is your favorite villain speech? And what can you learn from how the dialogue was constructed?

Look at the last three books you read, what kind of pressure was added to build the conflict?

What part of your favorite hero changes in order to beat the villain?

STEP 12 - Happily Never After - A Villain's Demise

Back To Class For A Spot Of Study

Endings with kisses at sunset from oil smothered muscly princes, surrounded by white unicorns and heart shaped balloons, are reserved for romance and kids' books only. Okay, maybe not kids' books unless you take away the oil and naked flesh otherwise... *Prison*. But seriously, romance novels and children's books are the only ones allowed to have enough happy-sparkles they make you want to vomit pink fluff.

In most other genres, unless it's carefully designed, having the villain lose everything and the hero live happily ever after isn't a credible ending. If you do that, readers will roll their eyes, chuck your book in the what-the-f**k-was-that-bucket and leave, never to return to your Amazon shelf again.

Now I'm not saying your hero shouldn't open a can of whoop-ass, secure the girl and save the world. He should, of course, and your can of whoop-ass should be overflowing with head-butts and villain ball breaks. But like I said in STEP 11, your hero needs to suffer for the win.

Nobody likes it when the villain rolls over and plays dead because little Tommy Tinkles finally stood up to him and said 'no.' Rip Tommy's fingers off, make him eat them for breakfast and *still* steal his lunch money. Then, and only then, can Tommy rise from his finger-less ashes and kick the big bully boy's balls.

This is important. Endings are specific. Genre specific. Readers stick to genres they love because, well, *they love them*. Just like kids stick to sugar and toy stores and spending all your bloody money because that's what they love.

Readers go back to a genre time and time again because they want to be told the same story, just in a new way. They are desperate for it; like it's book crack. I know it's weird, but it's also true. I can prove it. Take detective novels; every detective novel is *exactly* the same story:

Dead body appears. The detective hunts for clues. The detective finds clues. The detective solves the murder.

See? Told you.

Study your genre. Study like you're a seventeen-year-old boy, and your genre's the karma sutra: hard, fast and in serious detail. Knowing your genre's ending tropes will make your readers finish your book with a massive book hangover and come running back for more.

I'll assume you've read (and widely) your genre. If you haven't, stop reading this immediately. Get off your writer's butt and buy books. ALL. THE. BOOKS. Go. Study…

Examine the following:

- Where your genre puts their climaxes in relation to the ending.
- What happens to the villain?
- What happens to the hero?
- What happens to the minor characters?
- What themes are prevalent in the ending?
- What emotion are you left with?

Change Is Constant

My terror tot knows the pin code to my iPhone; he's better on the iPad than me, and your average six-year-old thinks Saw III is hilarious.

Life isn't like the old days. We're in this state of radical evolution that's exploding technology at an exponential rate. In ten years' time, the iPhone will look positively prehistoric compared to some totally augmented virtual reality mega terahertzy whatsit version eleventy point seven.

It's not just your genre you need to study, it's societal trends too. Take thrillers, 2012-2015 saw the rise of psychological thrillers with books like *Gone Girl* and *The Girl on the Train*. But already their popularity is waning, and soon a new type of genre twist will surface.

Whether you write Young Adult, New Adult or Adult Adult, there is one thing you can be sure of. Society will keep changing. We're media-monkeys and we're cannibalizing our brains with a junkie-like rate of consumption of crap TV and ever increasing special effects. We want bigger, better and more intelligent book endings.

Having a realistic ending is vital to creating a believable and satisfying conclusion for today's rather more voracious and impatient reader.

John Green's *The Fault in Our Stars* is an amazing example. Kids die. It's awful and harrowing, but it's true. The villain is intangible: childhood terminal illnesses. At the end of his book, we lose one kid to the villain, and although we're left with another, we know she's going to die too. It's gut-wrenchingly awful, but it's *also compelling, realistic and current.*

Happily Ever After (HEA) Or The Long And Boring View

Charming princes marrying princesses in Cinderella dresses and the knowledge that all the king's men *can* put Humpty together again is an HEA. It's your typical fairy tale ending where everyone's high on happiness, revolting displays of romance and sunsets. These endings are most common in romance stories and kids' books.

Happily Ever After From The Villain's POV

Sadly, your villain's screwed. This is the only ending where world domination of any kind is not on the cards. There will be no martinis, laughing and celebrations over the pressing of a big red button. Not this time, sorry, my evil friends.

The villain has to die.

The most important part of an HEA is that the villain dies *at the hand of your hero*.

The big bad super villain can't just trip over some debris mid-fight and impale himself on a sword. The only way to give a reader a satisfying ending is if Sir hero-a-lot kicks the villain into oblivion. Nothing else will do.

What Writers Need To Know

- The villain dies or is captured with no plausible way to return.

- The hero wins.

- The hero gets the girl.

- The world is happy forever more in its eye-achingly utopian bliss factory.

- The hero is happy living out a dreary married life with a gaggle of angelic hero children who also save the world as well as their children's children and so on forever. Until your readers are so saturated with generational heroism, childhood nightmares are vanquished forever.

If your readers are hero-worshipers, then HEA is the best reader oriented outcome. With HEAs, you round off all the story lines, leaving nothing unresolved. Readers know what happened to the hero, the villain, the cat, the dog's cousin, and the dustbin lid that got left atop a monk's head on a mountain eight chapters ago.

It is a simple fact of life that the older we get, the more life experience we have. That means HEAs are often less satisfying for adults.

A hero suddenly defeating the villain in the book's climax is not going to be believable or as satisfying as an ending where the hero only wins by the skin of his teeth.

Examples Of Happily Ever After

Happily ever after endings are found most often in children's fairy tales and more modern Disney and Pixar films.

- *Cinderella*
- *Sleeping Beauty*
- *Beauty and the Beast*
- *The Little Mermaid*
- *The Lion King*

HEAs are also found in romance books and films.

- *Pretty Woman*
- *Notting Hill*
- *Bridget Jones*
- Books by Jane Green and similarly some books by Lisa Jewell

Not-so Happily Ever After Ending

For the mass reading population, it's reasonable to suggest they read fiction for pleasure. Some read to escape their dreary corporate lives, others for fun and escapism.

Usually, but not always, not-so-happily ever after endings are found in literary fiction. This is often because the author is writing the story to make a point, an observation about society or creating some deeper philosophical discussion.

Not-so Happily Ever After From The Villain's POV

For the villain, this is the ending that results in him staring at the pearly gates of villain-heaven as villain-god opens the glorious golden metal grills and hands him a pair of angelic black wings for all eternity. **An ending that is not-so happily ever after simply means the villain wins. Or, everyone else dies.**

The important thing is the hero most definitely, does not win. Or if he does, he suffers such significant losses in the process, it wasn't worth it. In the film, *Assassin's Creed* Cal saves the magical apple but only because Maria (someone he cares about) sacrifices herself.

Although not the movie's finale, in *The Dark Knight,* one of the subplots involves Two-Face and Batman and the girl they both care deeply for: Rachel. Their mutual enemy at the time, the Joker, tricks both of them and kills her. Rachel's death is a not-so happily ever after ending and a huge win for the villain, because it's rare that the girl actually dies.

What Writers Need To Know

- The villain wins. Or if he doesn't win he gets away with something like Keyser Soze from *The Usual Suspects*, who gets away with a huge crime at the end of the film.

- The hero dies, or he survives, but a lot of the people the hero cares about die or get injured.

- Everybody in the book dies.

There is a health warning on this one because you still need to provide a satisfactory ending for your readers and if you kill off everyone, who will narrate the end of your story?

Above all, you need to foreshadow this ending early in your story because it's unusual and your reader won't expect it. So, if you don't foreshadow, they'll feel cheated.

That doesn't mean you need to give your plot's climax away, just do a Hansel and Gretel and leave foreshadow-like breadcrumbs in your chapters.

Examples Of Not-so Happily Ever After

Typically, this ending is found in horror films and horror books. One of the classic examples I remember watching when I was far too young is *Final Destination*. A girl had a premonition, saved a bunch of people, and then Death chased after them, killing each one in the order they should have died in the crash the girl foresaw.

Most books or films in the horror genre have this sort of ending.

- The *Halloween* movie series
- *Scream*
- *Texas Chainsaw Massacre*
- *Saw*

Other examples include the occasional mystery, thriller, literary fiction book or gangster related film.

- *Legend*
- *Seven*
- *The Usual Suspects*
- *Reservoir Dogs*

Other examples include literary fiction novel *The Beach* by Neville Shute and even the classic Shakespearean *Romeo and Juliet*.

The Hero's Sacrifice

The hero's sacrifice can come in many forms, but let's take the extreme view. The hero sacrifices their life to save everyone they love.

If you have written in a first person POV (point of view), this provides a problem. How do you write the end with no narrator? You could write it from the beyond, or use another character. Veronica Roth, the author of *Divergent*, does this, using the love interest to finish the story. You could also switch to a third person POV. But doing that suddenly can jar your reader out of the story unless you have periodically swapped POVs through the story. A.G. Howard, the author of the *Splintered* series, has used this technique in her book *RoseBlood*.

Howard uses one character to tell the story in the first person and another character in the third.

If you have more than one hero in your book, like George R.R. Martin in his *Song of Ice and Fire* series or even J.R.R. Tolkien in *The Lord of the Rings* then having hero sacrifices is easy, plausible and realistic.

The Hero's Sacrifice From The Villain's POV

Your villain will have put a number of obstacles in your hero's way to force the sacrifice. But death isn't the only option for your hero. It could be a minor sacrifice like giving up a piece of information, or it could be as serious as the choice in the book *Sophie's Choice* by William Styron where she has to choose which of her children will die.

The point is, even if your villain is defeated, he gets one up on the hero by making him sacrifice something. Or if the villain doesn't win outright, he wins in that the hero has to die to save everyone.

What Writers Need To Know

- The hero has to struggle against the villain throughout the story.

- The hero has to make a difficult choice.

- The hero has to sacrifice something important to them: something they love, need or a part of themselves.

- The hero's sacrifice must destroy the villain significantly enough he loses or dies.

More often than not the hero's sacrifice becomes a theme or a subplot of the book rather than the actual ending.

Most writers shy away from using a hero sacrifice because it closes off their story to any sequels.

On the flipside, it plays for a juicy character arc if your hero was selfish at the start and the arc makes him selfless enough to sacrifice himself. But usually, another character will come to the hero's aid, or he'll find a clever trick to defeat the villain without dying. Like in *The Hunger Games* where Katniss and Peeta agree to a suicide pact but President Snow stops it.

Examples Of A Hero's Sacrifice

You can find a hero's sacrifice in almost any genre, but often it's in anything where lots of action happens, for example, fantasy, thrillers, and also in young adult fiction.

- Tris Prior from *Allegiant* – the final book in the *Divergent* Trilogy
- Gandalf the Grey in *Lord of the Rings*
- Lots of characters in the *Game of Thrones* series
- Harry Potter, from *Harry Potter*.

Bittersweet - Twist

Bittersweet endings are my favorite. Perhaps the hardest one for a writer to compose, but the most satisfying to a reader.

These endings give readers a sick kind of pleasure. Like a gym-goer who's in agony from squatting too much weight, they feel the burn pulsing through their thighs, but carry on anyway because they're high on the endorphins. Bittersweet endings are the S and M version of a book ending because

they mix pleasure with pain.

Bittersweet endings are also synonymous with big plot twists because a twist gives you something unexpected and that's usually good and bad.

Bittersweet From The Villain's POV

Like the not so happily ever after, the villain might get what he wants in part, that's the 'bitter.' But there's still a sweet ending, so ultimately the hero will be victorious.

Example: Cruel Intentions, The Movie - The film *Cruel Intentions* has a bittersweet ending. It's a Young Adult romance story set in a private high school for rich kids.

The protagonist is a young girl called Annette who falls in love with your typical tall blond and handsome high school player, Sebastian.

The antagonist, Kathryn, is Sebastian's stepsister. In a twisted bet, Kathryn makes Sebastian chase after Annette. But the bet goes wrong, and he falls in love with Annette.

In the end, after Annette discovers the bet and breaks things off with Sebastian, he gives her his journal which details how he fell in love with her. Just as she finishes reading his journal, and finally believes he loves her, he gets run over and tragically dies.

Kathryn gets her comeuppance when she's caught taking drugs in school and loses

her prestigious head girl position as
well as her social circle and reputation.

What Writers Need To Know

- Loss, pain or regret should be key themes. The loss can't
  be small either. **You need to paint a proper pain-
  masterpiece. Take whatever the hero holds dearest
  and obliterate it.**

- **A bittersweet ending needs two things to happen to
  a hero: something positive and something negative.**

Examples Of A Bittersweet/Twist Ending

Bittersweet endings transcend genre fiction and by that I
mean they are universal and can be found in all genres. For
example, Young Adult fiction, chick flicks, and fantasy as well
as literary fiction.

- *The Fault in Our Stars* by John Greene
- *The Kite Runner* by Khaled Hosseini
- *Our Chemical Hearts* by K.M. Sutherland
- *My Husband's Wife* by Amanda Prowse

Ambiguous Endings

Ambiguous endings are often found in literary fiction,
mysteries, and any book series where there's a cliffhanger
ending because there's a sequel coming and likewise in films,
TV series, and soap operas.

The most obvious ambiguous ending is when the hero kills
the villain, but the reader's then given a clue to the villain's
surprise return in the next episode/film/series.

In literary fiction, and sometimes other genres, you can find endings where a subplot storyline is left open enough the reader has to infer or decide themselves what happened to the characters.

Ambiguous From The Villain's POV

This is one of the more exciting endings for a villain because he gets to play on. Usually, the villain will appear to have died or been defeated/imprisoned during the climax of the book. But additional footage after the credits or an epilogue might show a snippet of the villain's return.

What A Writer Needs To Know

There is a danger with ambiguous endings that readers are left unsatisfied with the outcome. Most readers don't like to make the ending up themselves. It's a risk.

If you leave an ending open, you need to make sure that every other subplot and storyline is 100% closed off with no possibility of an alternative outcome. And when I say closed off, I mean locked off tighter than Fort Knox.

Examples Of Ambiguous Endings

Usually found in literary fiction, or non-fiction if it's based on true life.

- *Goldfinch* by Donna Tartt
- *An Inspector Calls* by J.B. Priestly
- *Anne Frank* by Anne Frank (although her actual diaries are left ambiguous, recent publications have added information and research that tells the reader what happened to her after the diary entries finish)

- *The Shack* by W. M. Paul Young

STEP 12 – Happily Never After – A Villain's Demise Summary

Happy Ever After

- Your villain's stuffed. He has to die.

- The most important part of an HEA is that the villain dies at the hand of your hero.

Not-So Happily Ever After

- The important thing is the hero does not win. Or if he does, he suffers such significant losses in the process, it wasn't worth it.

- Above all, you need to foreshadow this ending earlier in your story. Because it's an unexpected ending your reader might feel cheated.

- That doesn't mean you need to give your plot's climax away, just do a Hansel and Gretel and leave breadcrumbs in your chapters.

Hero's Sacrifice

- Your villain should have put sufficient obstacles in your hero's way to result in her having to sacrifice something to win.

- More often than not the hero's sacrifice becomes more of a theme and a subplot rather than the actual book ending. Most writers shy away from using a hero sacrifice because it closes off their story to any sequels.

- Your biggest problem as a writer with this type of ending is finding a solution to who narrates the ending.

Bittersweet

- Bittersweet endings mix pleasure with pain.

- The hero needs to lose something significant, something that means the world to them. Whatever they lose needs to be significant enough it changes them forever.

- A bittersweet ending needs two things to happen to a hero: something positive and something negative.

Ambiguous Endings

- Mainly in literary fiction, but sometimes in other genres, you can find endings where a subplot storyline is left open enough that one of two possible outcomes could happen and it's for the reader to interpret and decide which ending happens.

- If you leave an ending open, you need to make sure that every other subplot and storyline is 100% closed off with no possibility of alternative outcomes.

Questions To Think About

What's the most common type of ending in your genre?

What's the best ending you ever read and why do you like it so much? What lesson or methodology can you take from that ending and use in your own work?

STEP 13 – Ending With An Introduction

It might seem odd to have this chapter at the end, but it's on purpose because introducing your villain is as important as creating the perfect first chapter hook.

If you don't know how to create a villain effectively, what's the point in knowing how to introduce him?

The villain's first appearance, like most factors, is genre dependent.

In some genres like mystery or crime, the bad guy's true identity stays secret until the last second. Instead the writer drop hints, clues and a flock of red herrings (although if you don't have at least one clue to who the villain is early on, the bad guy ends up holding no significance to the reader). In fantasy, it's equally important to show who the villain is as early as possible.

I'm not going to tell you exactly when you need to introduce your villain because there's no right or wrong answer. It's your prerogative as a writer to fit the entrance to your story.

However, there are some universal things about a villain's entrance.

Mystery And Mirrors

If you want to keep your villain's identity a secret, or even a mystery temporarily, there are certain things you have to do as a writer.

Diverting attention away from the villain isn't as easy as making the protagonist think someone else is the bad guy. In fact, if the protagonist places too much emphasis

on thinking another character is the villain, it's obvious to the reader that it's a red herring.

You also can't create a protagonist who is too dumb to work it out because that's unrealistic too.

Instead, have one or two characters that create doubt and raise questions. The characters should be dubious enough throughout your plot to cast doubt in both the reader and the protagonist's mind.

J.K. Rowling regularly hides true villains from the reader.

Example: Lord Voldemort character from Harry Potter and the Philosopher's Stone - Voldemort's presence is hidden in *Harry Potter and the Philosopher's Stone*. He hides under the turban of Professor Quirrell. Likewise, in *The Goblet of Fire*, Mad-Eye Moody has an impersonator hiding the villain's identity.

The Reader Is Einstein

As a writer, you need to assume all readers are the offspring of Einstein; *because they are.* They know everything: they were basically inside your head while you poured your story onto the page.

Your brain is see-through and as terrifying as it is, your every thought, every whimsical literary desire, is carved into your book's pages in Hollywood-sized neon writing. Your reader is a genius.

If you want an element of mystery around your villain, don't repeat information. Trust me; your reader picked up

on it the first time. Give clues in the subtlest way possible and choose your words carefully.

The Art Of Subtle

If you want to keep the villain a mystery, then hone your subtlety skills like a bumblebee zeroes in on a flower's delicious nectar.

Don't make your villain too righteous or saintly. Making them appear the exact opposite of what they are is a cliché, and your reader will see through it.

Likewise, don't make them too evil, because that's as obvious as a wallop to the crown jewels too. Like your mommy always said, everything in moderation, darling. That includes your villain.

The villain doesn't need to be in your face; it's just the concept of the villain that does.

Timing Is Everything

Think of your villain's introduction as a soufflé. Take your soufflé out of the oven too early, and the middle sinks. While it might still taste nice, you can't stop it looking like a crusty belly button.

Even if you want your villain to remain a secret until the end of your book, you need to introduce them, or the concept of them early on. After all, your whole plot is based on the relationship between your hero and villain.

Introducing them, however subtle, anywhere other than at the beginning of your story is a recipe for an unrealistic plot and your reader won't connect the dots. **Even if you want a**

big reveal, you still need the ground work and clues to weave through their subconscious during the plot, so the big reveal is both plausible and believable.

That doesn't mean you need to have your villain's physical body in the early chapters; allude to him or have the impact of his actions visible in those early chapters while other characters talk about him.

The reason you introduce the concept of your villain early on is so your reader knows what's at stake for your hero, and the thing that creates those stakes for your hero is the villain.

Whenever you introduce your villain, the most important aspect is to give your readers a sense of your villain's essence. Who is he? What is he about? How badly will he mess your hero up?

Example: The Dark Knight, The Movie - In *The Dark Knight*, the Joker is introduced early on in the film. Although we don't know who he is, to begin with because he's masked, we find out at the end of the closing scene.

The introduction scene involves a bank robbery by a group of masked robbers, of which the Joker is one. **There are two things we learn about the Joker:**

The first is that he is obscenely clever and that makes him highly dangerous. We know this because he orchestrated each of the gang members to shoot another leaving only him at the end with all the money and no eyewitnesses.

The second thing we learn which captures his essence is that he is a psychopath and utterly insane. One of the people that's shot during the robbery screams at the Joker and asks him what he believes in. The Joker rips off his mask displaying his bizarrely painted features and proclaims, *"Whatever doesn't kill you, makes you stranger."*

Here's a link to a clip of this scene: http://bit.ly/2iOqWkC

STEP 13 – Ending With An Introduction Summary

- Introducing the villain is genre dependent.

- Diverting attention away from the villain isn't as easy as making the protagonist think someone else is the bad guy. If you make the protagonist place too much emphasis on a character other than the villain, it becomes obvious to the reader he isn't your man.

- Instead, have one or two characters (or even an entire cast) that create doubt and raise questions.

- Assume your reader knows everything because, *they do*. Don't repeat information and give clues in a subtle way because readers are smart and pick up on everything.

- Don't make your villain too righteous or saintly. Making them appear the exact opposite of what they are is a cliché, and your reader will see through it.

- Likewise, don't make them too evil, because that's obvious too. Like your mommy always said, everything in moderation, darling. Including your villain.

- Even if you want a big reveal at the end of your book, you need to introduce your villain or the concept of him early on, so your reader's subconscious picks up on the clues, and the big reveal is both plausible and believable.

- Your villain doesn't need to be in your reader's face; it's just the concept of the villain that does.

- The reason you introduce the concept of your villain early on is that your reader needs to know what is at stake for your hero, and the thing that creates the stakes for your hero is the villain.

Questions To Think About

Think of your top five favorite books in your genre, which villain has the best introduction and why?

If the villain's in your genre aren't revealed until the end, how many breadcrumbs does the author drop and at what point in the story?

Piece It Like A Puzzle, Baby!

This is it. If you made it this far, then crack out the champers, baby, you did good. Not just because you listened to me ramble on for 40,000 words but because hopefully, you learned a thing or two about creating a darn good villain or should I say darn evil villain.

If I was Yoda, and this was *Star Wars*, then I'd be saying, "Master the apprentice has become." It's almost time for you to open your fledgling wings and flap off into the distant evil sunset.

I mean, it's as easy as piecing it all together and bleeding on the page, right? But to help you paint your innards into a shapely villain, I've created a checklist pulling out the key actions and questions you can't live without, which you can get here (http://eepurl.com/bRLqwT).

In the appendices, there are lists galore, including a list of famous villains you can analyze. Beauty, or maybe I mean villainy, is in the eye of the beholder. It's up to you to decide what's a good villain and what's a bad villain, but I hope that you base that decision on what you've learned, as well as the tropes of your genre and your market.

Go forth, villain masters and procreate your evilest children.

THANK YOU

Thank you for reading 13 Steps To Evil. I hope you found it helpful as you created your villain.

If you loved the book and can spare a few minutes, I would be really grateful for a short review on the site you purchased the book. Your support is appreciated.

If you would like to hear more about future publications or receive the checklist I mentioned as well as a free short course on villains, please sign up here.

http://eepurl.com/bRLqwT

Acknowledgements

Writers often see themselves as lone wolves, tapping away at the keyboard night after night. But it's not true. Not really. Every writer has a pack of wolves: friends, family, children, writing buddies, editors, designers and supporters, who group together and help an author to the finish line. Without them, this book would never have happened.

To my wife first, thank you for being so patient, for letting me follow my dream, and putting up with incessant tapping in the back of the living room. My son, for inspiring me to be a role model, and giving me the drive to show him you have to follow your dreams no matter what. Mum and Dad, thanks for, you know, doing it, and making an awesome kid.

My accountability partner, Allie Potts, for dragging my ass kicking and screaming to the finish line.

The Bloggers Bash committee, Ali, Geoff and Hugh, for the unending support and reassurance. I've no idea how you put up with me.

Suzie and Lucy, for listening to me on a daily basis and coaxing me off the cliff edge when my self-doubt reared its ugly head… Repeatedly.

My beta readers, Sarah, Ali, Lucy, Cynthia and Icy, your input was invaluable and has made this book so much better.

To my blogging friends, too many to mention, thank you for the continuous support, listening to my rambles, grumbles and excessive swearing!

To Dr. Amy Murphy, for years of friendship and for being the shrink I never could, thank you for correcting my rusty brain.

To the hundreds of writers, bloggers, friends and readers who filled out my research survey and made this book possible, I am indebted.

Last, and most importantly, thank you to you, the readers, for taking the time to buy and read this book. I hope it's been helpful, and I wish you success in your writing career.

About The Author

Sacha Black has five obsessions; words, expensive shoes, conspiracy theories, self-improvement, and breaking the rules. She also has the mind of a perpetual sixteen-year-old, only with slightly less drama and slightly more bills.

Sacha writes books about people with magical powers and other books about the art of writing. She lives in Hertfordshire, England, with her wife and genius, giant of a son.

When she's not writing, she can be found laughing inappropriately loud, blogging, sniffing musty old books, fangirling film and TV soundtracks, or thinking up new ways to break the rules.

Appendices

References

Personal learnings throughout six years of studying psychology:

1. First class Degree in Psychology
2. Masters in Research Methods in Cognitive Neuropsychology

Dr. Amy Murphy, Clinical Psychologist

www.dictionary.com

www.prisonreformtrust.org.uk/publications

The Psychology of Superheroes – An Unauthorized Exploration, Edited by Robin S. Rosenberg, PhD

As quoted in Einstein: The Man and His Achievement (1973) by G.J. Whitrow, p.42

Reel 421, Theodore Roosevelt papers, Manuscript Division, Library of Congress, Washington D.C

Further Reading

The Writer's Guide to Character Traits, by Dr. Linda N. Edelstein:

The Emotion Thesaurus by Angela Ackerman and Becca Puglisi:

The Negative Trait Thesaurus by Angela Ackerman and Becca Puglisi:

The Positive Trait Thesaurus by Angela Ackerman and Becca Puglisi:

The Psychology of Superheroes – An Unauthorized Exploration, Edited by Robin S. Rosenberg, PhD

The Writer's Guide To Psychology by Carolyn Kaufman

Appendices

Non-Exhaustive List Of Fictional Book And Movie Villains

1. Dracula from *Dracula*
2. Vito Corleone from the *Godfather*
3. Freddy Krueger from *A Nightmare on Elm Street*
4. Jack Colby from *High Noon*
5. Ernst Stavro Blofeld from *You Only Live Twice*
6. Jud Casper from *Kes*
7. Iago from *Othello*
8. Darth Vader from *Star Wars*
9. Annie Wilkes from *Misery*
10. Red Grant from *Russia With Love*
11. Alex Forrest from *Fatal Attraction*
12. Travis Bickle from *Taxi Driver*
13. Colonel Walter E. Kurtz from *Apocalypse Now*
14. The Child Catcher from *Chitty Chitty Bang Bang*
15. The Joker from *The Dark Knight*
16. Bane from *The Dark Knight Rises*
17. Alex DeLarge from *A Clockwork Orange*
18. Lord Voldemort from *Harry Potter and The Philosopher's Stone*
19. The Monster from *Frankenstein*
20. Norman Bates from *Psycho*
21. The Wicked Witch of the West from *The Wizard of Oz*
22. Tommy DeVito from *Goodfellas*
23. Richard III from *Richard III*
24. Amon Goeth from *Schindler's List*
25. Nurse Ratched from *One Flew Over the Cuckoo's Nest*

26. Hannibal Lecter from *Silence of The Lambs*
27. Joan Crawford from *Mummy Dearest*
28. Gunnery Sgt Hartman from *Full Metal Jacket*
29. The Evil Queen from *Snow White and The Seven Dwarfs*
30. Cruella De Ville from *101 Dalmatians*
31. The Sheriff of Nottingham from *Robin Hood*
32. Leatherface from *Texas Chainsaw Massacre*
33. Keyser Soze from *The Usual Suspects*
34. Hans Gruber from *Die Hard*
35. Hans Landa from *Inglorious Bastards*
36. Jack Torrance from *The Shining*
37. Clarence Boddicker from *Robocop*
38. General Zod from *Superman II*
39. Michael Myers from *Halloween*
40. Anton Chigurh from *No Country for Old Men*
41. John Doe from *Seven*
42. Auric Goldfinger from *Goldfinger*
43. HAL 9000 from *2001 A Space Odyssey*
44. The Alien from *Alien*
45. T-1000 from *Terminator 2: Judgement Day*
46. Agent Smith from *The Matrix*
47. Gordon Gecko from *Wall Street*
48. Dudley Smith from *LA Confidential*
49. Frank Booth from *Blue Velvet*
50. Ivan Drago from *Rocky*
51. Begbie from *Trainspotting*
52. Russ Cargill from *The Simpsons Movie*
53. Davy Jones from *Pirates of the Caribbean*
54. Captain Barbossa from *Pirates of the Caribbean*
55. Count Olaf from the *Lemony Snicket - A Series of Unfortunate Events*

56. The Green Goblin from *Spider-Man*
57. President Snow from *The Hunger Games* by Suzanne Collins
58. Amy Dunne from *Gone Girl*
59. Tom Ripley from *The Talented Mr. Ripley*
60. Moriarty from *The Final Problem* by Sir Arthur Conan Doyle
61. Steerpike from *Titus Groan and Gormenghast* by Mervyn Peake
62. Shere Khan from *The Jungle Book* by Rudyard Kipling
63. The White Witch from *The Lion, The Witch and The Wardrobe* by C.S. Lewis
64. Milo Minderbinder from *Catch 22* by Joseph Heller
65. Fred from the *Handmaid's Tale* by Margaret Atwood
66. Grendel's Mother from *Beowulf*
67. O'Brien from *Nineteen Eighty-Four* by George Orwell
68. Captain Hook from *Peter And Wendy* by J.M. Barrie
69. Ms Coulter from *His Dark Materials* trilogy by Philip Pullman
70. Clare Quilty from *Lolita* by Vladimir Nabokov
71. Bill Sykes from *Oliver Twist* by Charles Dickens
72. Sauron from *The Lord of the Rings* by J.R.R. Tolkien
73. Mr. Hyde from *The Strange Case of Dr. Jekyll and Mr. Hyde,* by Robert Louis Stevenson
74. Satan from *Paradise Lost* by John Milton

Non-Exhaustive List Of Anti-heroes

1. Beetlejuice from *Beetlejuice*
2. Deadpool
3. Suicide squad
4. Jordan Belfort from *The Wolf of Wall Street*
5. Jason Bourne from the *Jason Bourne* movies based on the books by Robert Ludlum
6. Chev Chelios from *Crank*
7. John Constantine from *Constantine*
8. Judge Dredd from *Dredd*
9. Hellboy from *Hellboy*
10. Jack Reacher from the *Jack Reacher* series
11. Shrek from *Shrek*
12. Captain Jack Sparrow from *Pirates of the Carribean*
13. V from *V for Vendetta*
14. Theodore 'T-Bag' Bagwell from *Prison Break*
15. Jack Bauer from *24*
16. Edmund Blackadder from the BBC's *Blackadder* series
17. Chuck Bass from *Gossip Girl*
18. Nicholas Brody from *Homeland*
19. Saul Goodman from *Better Call Saul* and *Breaking Bad*
20. Jimmy McNulty from *The Wire*
21. Dexter Morgan from *Dexter*
22. Tony Soprano from *The Sopranos*
23. Walter White from *Breaking Bad*
24. Magneto and Wolverine from the *X-men*
25. Patrick Bateman from *American Psycho*
26. Miranda Priestly from *The Devil Wears Prada*

Traits

Positive Traits

Accessible	Ebullient	Logical	Scholarly
Active	Educated	Lovable	Scrupulous
Adaptable	Efficient	Loyal	Secure
Admirable	Elegant	Lyrical	Selfless
Adventurous	Eloquent	Magnanimous	Self-critical
Agreeable	Empathetic	Many-sided	Self-denying
Alert	Energetic	Masculine (or feminine)	Self-reliant
Allocentric	Enthusiastic	Mature	Self-sufficient
Amiable	Exciting	Methodical	Sensitive
Anticipative	Extraordinary	Meticulous	Sentimental
Appreciative	Fair	Moderate	Seraphic
Articulate	Faithful	Modest	Serious
Aspiring	Farsighted	Multileveled	Sexy
Athletic	Felicific	Neat	Sharing
Attractive	Firm	Non-authoritarian	Shrewd
Balanced	Flexible	Objective	Simple
Benevolent	Focused	Observant	Skilful
Brilliant	Forceful	Open	Sober
Calm	Forgiving	Optimistic	Sociable

Capable	Forthright	Orderly	Solid
Captivating	Freethinking	Organized	Sophisticated
Caring	Friendly	Original	Spontaneous
Challenging	Fun-loving	Painstaking	Sporting
Charismatic	Gallant	Passionate	Stable
Charming	Generous	Patient	Steadfast
Cheerful	Gentle	Patriotic	Steady
Clean	Liberal	Sane	Stoic
Clear-headed	Genuine	Peaceful	Strong
Clever	Good-natured	Perceptive	Studious
Colorful	Gracious	Perfectionist	Suave
Companion	Hardworking	Personable	Subtle
Compassionate	Healthy	Persuasive	Sweet
Conciliatory	Hearty	Planner	Sympathetic
Confident	Helpful	Playful	Systematic
Conscientious	Heroic	Polished	Tasteful
Considerate	High-minded	Popular	Teacher
Constant	Honest	Practical	Thorough
Contemplative	Honorable	Precise	Tidy
Cooperative	Humble	Principled	Tolerant
Courageous	Humorous	Profound	Tractable
Courteous	Idealistic	Protean	Trusting

Creative	Imaginative	Protective	Uncomplaining
Cultured	Impressive	Providential	Understanding
Curious	Incisive	Prudent	Undogmatic
Daring	Incorruptible	Punctual	Unfoolable
Debonair	Independent	Purposeful	Upright
Decent	Individualistic	Rational	Urbane
Decisive	Innovative	Realistic	Venturesome
Dedicated	Inoffensive	Reflective	Vivacious
Deep	Insightful	Relaxed	Warm
Dignified	Insouciant	Reliable	Well-bred
Directed	Intelligent	Resourceful	Well-read
Disciplined	Intuitive	Respectful	Well-rounded
Discreet	Invulnerable	Responsible	Winning
Dramatic	Kind	Reverential	Wise
Dutiful	Knowledgeable	Romantic	Witty
Dynamic	Leader	Rustic	Youthful
Earnest	Leisurely	Sage	

Negative Traits

Abrasive	Disruptive	Messy	Sloppy
Abrupt	Dissolute	Miserable	Slow
Agonizing	Dissonant	Miserly	Sly
Aggressive	Distractible	Misguided	Small-thinking
Aimless	Disturbing	Mistaken	Softheaded
Airy	Dogmatic	Money-minded	Sordid
Aloof	Domineering	Monstrous	Steely
Amoral	Dull	Moody	Stiff
Angry	Easily Discouraged	Morbid	Strong-willed
Anxious	Egocentric	Muddle-headed	Stupid
Apathetic	Enervated	Naive	Submissive
Arbitrary	Envious	Narcissistic	Superficial
Argumentative	Erratic	Narrow	Superstitious
Arrogant	Escapist	Narrow-minded	Tactless
Artificial	Excitable	Natty	Tasteless
Asocial	Expedient	Negativistic	Tense
Assertive	Extravagant	Neglectful	Thievish
Astigmatic	Extreme	Neurotic	Thoughtless
Authoritarian	Faithless	Nihilistic	Timid
Barbaric	False	Obnoxious	Transparent

Bewildered	Fanatical	Obsessive	Treacherous
Bizarre	Fanciful	Obvious	Trendy
Bland	Fatalistic	Odd	Troublesome
Blunt	Fawning	Offhand	Unappreciative
Boisterous	Fearful	One-dimensional	Uncaring
Brittle	Fickle	One-sided	Uncharitable
Brutal	Fiery	Opinionated	Unconvincing
Business-like	Fixed	Opportunistic	Uncooperative
Calculating	Flamboyant	Oppressed	Uncreative
Callous	Foolish	Outrageous	Uncritical
Cantankerous	Forgetful	Over-imaginative	Unctuous
Careless	Fraudulent	Paranoid	Undisciplined
Cautious	Frightening	Passive	Unfriendly
Charmless	Frivolous	Pedantic	Ungrateful
Childish	Gloomy	Perverse	Unhealthy
Clumsy	Graceless	Petty	Unimaginative
Coarse	Grand	Phlegmatic	Unimpressive
Cold	Greedy	Plodding	Unlovable
Colorless	Grim	Pompous	Unmotivated
Complacent	Gullible	Possessive	Unpolished
Complaintive	Hateful	Power-hungry	Unprincipled

Compulsive	Haughty	Predatory	Unrealistic
Conceited	Hedonistic	Prejudiced	Unreflective
Condemnatory	Hesitant	Presumptuous	Unreliable
Confidential	Hidebound	Pretentious	Unrestrained
Conformist	High-handed	Prim	Non-self-critical
Confused	Hostile	Procrastinating	Unstable
Contemptible	Ignorant	Profligate	Vacuous
Conservative	Imitative	Provocative	Vague
Conventional	Impatient	Pugnacious	Venal
Cowardly	Imprudent	Puritanical	Venomous
Crafty	Impulsive	Quirky	Vindictive
Crass	Inconsiderate	Reactionary	Vulnerable
Crazy	Incurious	Reactive	Weak
Criminal	Indecisive	Regimental	Weak-willed
Critical	Indulgent	Regretful	Well-meaning
Crude	Inert	Monstrous	Willful
Cruel	Inhibited	Repentant	Wishful
Cynical	Insecure	Repressed	Zany
Decadent	Insensitive	Resentful	
Deceitful	Insincere	Ridiculous	
Delicate	Insulting	Rigid	
Demanding	Intolerant	Ritualistic	

Dependent	Irascible	Rowdy	
Desperate	Irrational	Ruined	
Destructive	Irresponsible	Sadistic	
Devious	Irritable	Sanctimonious	
Difficult	Lazy	Scheming	
Dirty	Libidinous	Scornful	
Disconcerting	Loquacious	Secretive	
Discontented	Malicious	Sedentary	
Discouraging	Mannered	Selfish	
Dishonest	Manner-less	Self-indulgent	
Disloyal	Mawkish	Shallow	
Disobedient	Mealy-mouthed	Short-sighted	
Disorderly	Mechanical	Shy	
Disorganized	Meddlesome	Silly	
Disputatious	Melancholic	Single-minded	
Disrespectful	Meretricious		

Neutral Traits

Absentminded	Emotional	Non-competitive	Stern
Ambitious	Enigmatic	Obedient	Stolid
Amusing	Experimental	Old-fashioned	Strict
Artful	Familial	Ordinary	Stubborn
Ascetic	Folksy	Outspoken	Stylish
Authoritarian	Formal	Paternalistic	Subjective
Big-thinking	Freewheeling	Physical	Surprising
Boyish	Frugal	Placid	Soft
Breezy	Glamorous	Political	Tough
Business-like	Guileless	Predictable	Unaggressive
Busy	High-spirited	Preoccupied	Unambitious
Casual	Hurried	Private	Unceremonious
Cerebral	Hypnotic	Progressive	Unchanging
Chummy	Iconoclastic	Proud	Undemanding
Circumspect	Idiosyncratic	Pure	Unfathomable
Competitive	Impassive	Questioning	Unhurried

Complex	Impersonal	Quiet	Uninhibited
Confidential	Impressionable	Religious	Unpatriotic
Contradictory	Intense	Reserved	Unpredictable
Crisp	Invisible	Restrained	Unreligious
Cute	Irreligious	Retiring	Unsentimental
Deceptive	Irreverent	Sarcastic	Whimsical
Determined	Maternal	Self-conscious	Stern
Dominating	Mellow	Sensual	Stolid
Dreamy	Modern	Sceptical	Strict
Droll	Moralistic	Smooth	Stubborn
Dry	Mystical	Soft	Stylish
Earthy	Neutral	Solemn	Subjective
Effeminate	Noncommittal	Solitary	Surprising

List Of Core Values

Positive Values

Authenticity	Courage	Health	Security
Accountability	Creativity	Honesty	Self-respect
Achievement	Curiosity	Humor	Spirituality
Adventure	Dependability	Independence	Stability
Attractiveness	Determination	Integrity	Strength
Authenticity	Discipline	Justice	Success
Balance	Efficiency	Kindness	Support
Challenge	Enthusiasm	Knowledge	Trustworthiness
Clarity	Ethics	Leadership	Vision
Commitment	Excellence	Love	Wisdom
Communication	Fairness	Loyalty	
Compassion	Flexibility	Openness	
Competitiveness	Freedom	Optimism	
Competency	Friendship	Pleasure	
Confidence	Generosity	Persistence	
Continuous learning or growth	Happiness	Respect	

List Of Negative Values

Anger or Rage	Fame	Inequality	Self-doubt
Anxiety	Fear	Lethargy	Sorrow
Bitterness	Frustration	Loneliness	Status
Condemnation	Gloom	Misery	Suspicion
Criticizing others	Greed	Ostracism	Withdrawal
Cynicism	Guilt	Pessimism	Worry
Depression	Helplessness	Pleasure	
Despair	Hostility	Regret	
Despondency	Humiliation	Rejection	
Discouraging	Jealousy	Resignation	
Disinterested	Judgmental	Rigidity	
Failure	Illness	Sadness	

List Of Soul Scars

Saved someone's life	Failed	Victim of crime	Involved in a Cult
Survived a car crash	Failed Continually	Surgery	Lost religious belief
Lost a limb during a war	Failed exams	Addiction	Witnessed cruelty or crime and weren't able to help
Never making it to a loved one's deathbed	Had to care for a loved one long term	Raped	Experienced a natural disaster
Divorced	Neglected as a child	Miscarried	Tornado
Abandoned - by parents / lover / siblings	Terminal illness	Death of a child	Hurricane
Rejected by loved ones	Lied to	Toxic Friendship	Earthquake
Unrequited love	Being cheated on	Fell out of or lost friends	Tsunami

Bullied	Lied to about your parentage or familial line/heritage	Crossed a moral line to survive	Sacked
Abused by parents / spouse	Was adopted	Broke the law for the right reason	Period of mental illness
Manipulated	Long period of unemploymen t	Made redundant	Depression
Death of a loved one	Kidnapped		

Printed in Great Britain
by Amazon